"The Apostle Paul kne[w]
integrating examples f[...]
moments from one of college football's greatest rivalries to stir readers to think about biblical truth. Fans will no doubt enjoy reliving some of the great moments of Auburn football history, but with a fresh perspective, considering there are lessons to be learned from these occasions."

—Bob Crittenden, host,
The Meeting House, Faith Radio in Alabama

"Auburn Tiger football has a storied history of team success and individual greatness. Author Del Duduit shares this great history and incorporates an inspiring Christian message along the way. Football and faith are a great combination."

—Cary Knox, author, inspirational
speaker, teacher, and coach

"For college football fans outside of the SEC, it is just a game. But, to the Tigers, the Iron Bowl is just as important as a National Championship. Del uses this long-standing rivalry to focus in on the battle in our faith where 'iron sharpens iron.' Read some of the great gridiron moments for Auburn while sharpening your faith for your own spiritual playbook."

—Ben Cooper, author and speaker.

"*Auburn Believer* goes deep with practical wisdom and nostalgia as Del Duduit converts Auburn football's greatest moments into a winning devotional for Tiger fans of all ages."

—Doug Carter, professor and writer

"If life, we must all hire on and do the work we were hired to do. If you're an Auburn University student, your job is to learn and grow. If you're an Auburn athlete, your job is to be a student, a leader, and a contributor. As Christians, we are hired on to spread the good news of Christ's gospel message. *Auburn Believer* allows you to celebrate all things Auburn and develop the God-honoring skills you need to 'Ride the Brand' and make a difference in this world for God."

—J. D. Wininger, caretaker at
Cross-Dubya Ranch and author

AUBURN BELIEVER

40 DAYS OF DEVOTIONS FOR THE TIGER FAITHFUL

DEL DUDUIT

IRON STREAM
BOOKS

An imprint of Iron Stream Media
Birmingham, Alabama

Other books in the Stars of the Faith Series

Dugout Devotions: Inspirational Hits from MLB's Best
First Down Devotions: Inspiration from NFL's Best
Bama Believer: 40 Days of Devotions for the Roll Tide Faithful

Iron Stream Books
100 Missionary Ridge
Birmingham, AL 35242
IronStreamMedia.com
Iron Stream Books is an imprint of Iron Stream Media

Library of Congress Control Number: 2019955617

Unless otherwise indicated, all Scripture quotations are from The Holy Bible, English Standard Version® (ESV®), copyright © 2001 by Crossway, a publishing ministry of Good News Publishers. Used by permission. All rights reserved.

Scripture quotations marked (KJV) are taken from The Holy Bible, King James Version.

Scripture quotations marked (NKJV) are taken from the New King James Version®. Copyright © 1982 by Thomas Nelson. Used by permission. All rights reserved.

ISBN-13: 978-1-56309-370-8
Ebook ISBN: 978-1-56309-371-5
1 2 3 4 5—24 23 22 21 20

This book is dedicated to all Tiger fans and those who appreciate good football and faith.

CONTENTS

ACKNOWLEDGMENTS

Several people played a key role in making this book a reality. I would like to thank the following for their efforts in bringing *Auburn Believer: 40 Days of Devotions for the Tiger Faithful* to you.

- ➢ My wife Angie for being the initial editor of this book and for her support.

- ➢ My agent Cyle Young for his work to get it in front of the right publisher.

- ➢ My publisher John Herring for his trust in me.

- ➢ My associate publisher Ramona Richards for her encouragement.

- ➢ My production crew and cheerleaders, Meredith Dunn and Tina Atchenson, at Iron Stream Media.

- ➢ My final editor Reagan Jackson for her wonderful eye and making this book better.

- ➢ My Lord and Savior for this exciting opportunity.

DAY 1
GO OVER THE TOP FOR GOD

November 27, 1982: Auburn 23, Alabama 22

And whatever you do, in word or deed, do everything
in the name of the Lord Jesus, giving thanks to God the
Father though him. —Colossians 3:17

In 1982, the last time Auburn had defeated Alabama in the Iron
Bowl was 1972.

A win was needed to break the nine-year losing skid to
their state rival.

The Tide rolled first into the end zone when quarterback
Walter Lewis found wide receiver Joey Jones for a twenty-two-
yard score.

Alabama was in prime position to increase the lead when
Tiger safety Mark Dorminey hit running back Joe Carter at the
Auburn fifteen-yard line and forced a fumble. Tim Drinkard
picked up the pigskin and returned it sixty-two-yards to the
Bama thirteen-yard line.

Auburn running back Lionel James took the handoff and
romped the distance to tie the game 7–7.

A field goal put Alabama ahead 10–7, but that did not last
long.

Auburn safety Bob Harris picked off a pass from Lewis and put the Tigers in scoring position.

Quarterback Randy Campbell crossed the goal line from three yards out to boost the Tigers to a 14–10 lead.

Another Alabama field goal cut the deficit to 14–13 at the break.

The second half started right for Alabama as they drove sixty-six yards in eight plays and culminated when running back Paul Ott Carruth scored from eight yards out. A third field goal boosted the Tide lead to 22–14 toward the end of the third quarter.

The Tigers cut into the lead when Al Del Greco connected for a field goal. But time was running out.

Campbell led Auburn down the field, and running back Bo Jackson was stopped eighteen inches from the goal line with two minutes and thirty seconds to play.

Bo Jackson, a freshman, was an incredible athlete and a six-foot-nine high jumper in high school. He suggested to coach Pat Dye that he "go over the top" with the ball.

Lead blockers went first to make way for Jackson, who leaped over the line and into the end zone for the score and the 23–22 win.

The losing skid was over, and Auburn fans stormed Legion Field to tear down the goal posts. Coach Dye was picked up and carried off the field on the shoulders of his players.

Have you ever gone over the top for the Lord? Do you have confidence in your relationship with God to plunge into the end zone?

Day 1: Go Over the Top for God

Only fear the LORD and serve him faithfully with all your heart. For consider what great things he has done for you. —1 Samuel 12:24

WAR EAGLE

What do you do to show others Christ lives in you? Are you willing to dive over the line for the touchdown? Perhaps you are living a successful life and are doing the right things. You hold down a good job and have a wonderful family who goes to church together. Or maybe it's the other way around, and you struggle to make ends meet. You have personal issues and often battle the forces of evil that want to make a goal-line stand. Get into the huddle in prayer, and make the decision to go over the top.

RIDE FOR THE BRAND

No matter what you face in life, you can be bold enough in your relationship to trust God to make a way for you to dive into the end zone. You might be faced with a job loss or receive disturbing news from your doctor that catches you off guard. Everyone has triumphs and losses, but you have a Coach who will design the winning play and help you break the losing streak. Here are some suggestions to consider for you to dive over the top every day:

> ➢ Serve Others: Make an effort to get to know those you come into contact with each day. Everyone has a story and their own personal struggles. Relationships are

meant to be cultivated and groomed. Take time to find out what people are going through. Volunteer at a soup kitchen or spend a few hours a month at a hospice unit or the hospital. Once you know their stories, you can be of service and a blessing. Your opinions and outlooks might change for the better. "For the whole law is fulfilled in one word: 'You shall love your neighbor as yourself'" (Galatians 5:14).

➢ Thirst for Wisdom: You cannot rely on your pastor or Sunday school teachers to provide all of this for you. Football players need helmets and equipment to perform well. You too need guidance from God to be a winner. You must seek the Lord's will in your life and spend time in the Word. Auburn players knew the playbook and how to execute assignments. The same goes for you. Apply God's Word in your life each day. "How much better to get wisdom than gold! To get understanding is to be chosen rather than silver" (Proverbs 16:16).

➢ Cultivate a Forgiving Heart: This can be a challenge. But you have to be like Auburn's offense and jump over the Bama line of defense. Forgiveness must be accompanied by the grace that only God can give you. Apply this with compassion every day. For instance: The neighbor who borrowed your weed trimmer and hasn't returned it yet, the person who cut you off in traffic, or the friend who stood you up for lunch. Never expect anything in return, and opt to love those who don't treat you well. Show forgiveness.

Day 1: Go Over the Top for God

➢ Show Gratitude: Your life might not be going as you planned, but remember God is in control. He may not want you to have that promotion because it might make you spend too much time away from your family. He might not allow you to buy that big boat you've been dreaming about because it could interfere with your church attendance. Maybe He has something better planned for you. Be happy and content with the blessings the Master has given you. Dreams are fine to have, but be satisfied with your relationship with Christ.

➢ Worship the Lord: If your sins have been washed by the blood of Jesus and you are on your way to heaven, you have a right to lift your hands and stand to your feet to praise Him. This can be done in church, at home, or even in public. You won't think twice about cheering on the Tigers when they make a touchdown, and that's awesome. But remember you are on the winning team in the game of life. Take the time to praise God for all the wonderful things He has done for you.

Bo Jackson believed in his ability to plunge into the end zone for the score. He used his talent to lead his team to victory. You can do the same each day in your walk with the Lord. Go over the top!

DAY 2
MAKE THE COMEBACK

November 26, 2010: Auburn 28, Alabama 27

Trust in the LORD will all thine heart; and lean not unto thine own understanding. —Proverbs 3:5 KJV

The task was insurmountable. No team had ever come back from an Alabama twenty-four-point lead.

It was unheard of.

Until the 2010 Iron Bowl.

The Tide rolled to a twenty-four-point lead in the first half, and any hopes of an Auburn National Championship, as well as a Heisman Trophy for quarterback Cam Newton, were fading fast.

But the Tigers had a knack for coming from behind and winning the game. In eight out of the twelve games played during the season, Auburn had trailed—but never by this much.

Newton, who was on pace to grab college football's most prestigious award, led a dramatic comeback.

He bolted into the end zone from a yard out and fired a thirty-six-yard touchdown pass to Emory Blake to reduce the deficit.

The number-two ranked Tigers got another touchdown pass from Newton, this time a whopping seventy-yarder to

Terrell Zachery, followed by a seven-yard strike to Philip Lutzenkirchen at the start of the fourth quarter to give Auburn its first lead of the day.

The one-hundred-thousand-plus people in the stands in Tuscaloosa, Alabama, sat stunned and knew something was different with this Tiger team, which was not about to quit and roll over.

Auburn had trailed Alabama 21–0 before they even picked up a first down. But the most overwhelming statistic of the Tide's early dominance was when they outgained Auburn 314 yards to only two.

It's no wonder the Auburn fans were disheartened and thought the game was over. But it was also a defining moment for Newton who took matters into his own hands and willed the team to make the dramatic come-from-behind win.

Auburn would go on to win the National Championship when it knocked off Oregon 22–19, and Newton captured the Heisman Trophy.

But at one time, during the Alabama game, those accomplishments were in extreme jeopardy.

Just when the situation looked grim, Auburn reached down and found a way to win the Iron Bowl.

Have you ever made a dramatic comeback? Maybe you have been down in the score and things looked bleak for you.

In all thy ways acknowledge him, and he shall direct thy paths. —Proverbs 3:6 KJV

Day 2: Make the Comeback

WAR EAGLE

Have you ever been discouraged as a follower of the Lord? Perhaps you have been injured by someone's words or have been betrayed by a person you trusted. Maybe you were wronged by an individual in your church or community or you may be the one who hurt someone else. No matter what has happened, circumstances have caused you to drift in your relationship with the Lord. Before you know it, you are down 24–0, and nothing is going right. You started off your journey with a bang and were undefeated. You had aspirations of winning God's National Title and ending up in the winners' circle in heaven. Now, it's all in jeopardy. The devil has you right where he wants you—losing the game and watching the entire season become flooded with doubt.

RIDE FOR THE BRAND

You are better than this. Everyone has issues and problems and can easily fall into a rut. Discouragement is a powerful tool used by Satan. He will put things into your life to tempt you to cut back on your daily Bible reading and prayer. He will toss in important activities that draw you away from church. And he will put bitterness and other ill feelings into your heart. This puts you down in the count and makes the outcome seem hopeless. But just like Cam did, you must take matters into your own hands and make a statement that you will lead the charge to post a dramatic comeback. Here are some suggestions to come from behind for the win with Christ:

Auburn Believer

➤ Realize the Situation: The game of life can quickly overwhelm you and cause you to confuse your priorities. But you must recognize what is about to happen before it gets out of hand. You need to adapt to the situation, just like Auburn did, and make adjustments. When you see a pattern that is taking you the wrong way, then put an end to it immediately. You don't want to find yourself in a situation where you could embarrass yourself or your family's reputation. Trust God to steer you in the right direction.

➤ Put Aside Your Ego: Pride can bring you down fast, and humility is essential in your Christian walk. When you realize a circumstance is beyond your control, then toss the ego to the curb and ask God for help. A man is strongest when he's on his knees in prayer. "But he giveth more grace. Wherefore he saith, God resisteth the proud, but giveth grace unto the humble" (James 4:6 KJV).

➤ Realize What Is at Stake: When you allow the devil to take a big lead on you before the half, you can lose more than a game. The Tigers had a lot on the line: an undefeated season, a possible National Title, and a Heisman Trophy candidate. A loss surely would have hurt the chances for all three to occur. You also have a lot at stake: your job, your family, your reputation, your eternal salvation. When you find yourself behind in the game, you have to weigh the costs. Is meeting a person for dinner when you know it's wrong worth the consequences? Is taking that job promotion that might take time away from your family really worth the extra money? Is avoiding a personal conviction worth the risk of damaging your reputation in the community? Once you see the price tag on the shiny temptation from the devil, you will see how he's hiding the problems that come along with his lies. This doesn't mean you should never seek a promotion, but you must weigh the pros and cons for you and your loved ones. Decisions have results, and actions have consequences. Examine them carefully and ask God for His direction. "I will instruct thee and teach thee in the way which thou shalt go: I will guide thee with mine eye" (Psalm 32:8 KJV).

➤ Seek the Lord: Call on the name of Christ, and He will lead you in your journey. Cam Newton took matters into his own hands, and the team came out a winner. You must turn the reigns over to the Master and allow Him to make the calls in the huddle. Pray hard, and let Him speak to you through his Word.

➤ Make the Go-Ahead Score: You can make the big play to bring your team to victory. Winning a rivalry game is not easy, and it takes trust in your teammates. Confide in your church family or close friends, who can offer moral support and prayer. When the game clock is over and you have posted the most points, you all can celebrate the big win together.

Life can come up on you fast and post a big score before the half. But when you realize the situation and toss aside the ego and ask God for help, you will put yourself in a position to make the come-from-behind win.

DAY 3
STOMP OUT THE BITTERNESS

February 22, 1893: Auburn 32, Alabama 22

See to it that no one fails to obtain the grace of God; that
no "root of bitterness" springs up and causes trouble, and
by it many become defiled. —Hebrews 12:15

The rivalry between Auburn and Alabama started on the
gridiron in 1893 and has developed into one of the most heated
in college football.

The state is divided, and the two schools are separated
by about a three-hour drive. The rivalry has become even
more intense because of Alabama's overall success over the
past decade. Together the two programs hold thirty-five
Southeastern Conference titles and nineteen national champi-
onships. And those numbers are sure to grow.

But the famous feud did not even begin on the football
field. It actually got its start in the Alabama State Legislature
during the Civil War Reconstruction Era, originating with a
dispute over the location of a new land-grant college. A debate
that lasted for four years ended with Auburn as the winning
site in 1872. Auburn continued to be a political football over
the years due to a state legislature stacked with many Alabama

alumni, and bitter feelings between the two schools continued for decades going forward.

Consequently, the first football game between the adversaries took on more meaning than just an athletic contest played in front of about five thousand people at Birmingham's Lakeview Park. There were intense emotions woven throughout the matchup.

Auburn's R. T. Dorsey scored three touchdowns and Tom Daniels added two scores as the Tigers controlled the Tide and won the game 32–22.

Let all bitterness and wrath and anger and clamor and slander be put away from you, along with all malice.
—Ephesians 4:31

WAR EAGLE

It doesn't take much today to cause ill feelings between people. An argument or a disagreement from years past can take its toll on a relationship. I remember I lost a friend when I coached Little League All-Stars two decades ago. Against my gut instinct, I added my friend's son to the team and explained that the boy would receive the minimal time allowed. He said it was okay and thanked me for putting the young man on the roster. Halfway through the tournament, this dad became furious with me because his son was not playing as much as he thought he should. I reminded him of the agreement and continued to coach. He refused to speak to me, and our relationship was strained. Perhaps you have an issue with someone that you wished never happened. How have you handled the circumstance? The smallest match can ignite a tremendous fire if it's allowed to breathe and gain strength. Put out the flames.

RIDE FOR THE BRAND

There are ways for a believer of the gospel to mend a broken relationship and douse the fires of bitterness. This process isn't easy, but you should consider the following steps if you suffer from a strained relationship or from "political" decisions from your past:

➤ Talk to God First: Seek His wisdom and direction before you try to talk to a person about a conflict. Consult with the Lord, and ask Him to prepare your heart and mind.

➤ Take the First Step: Don't let time gather momentum and enlarge the barrier between you and the other party involved. Time has a way of getting out of control if left unattended. When God gives you the green light, step on the pedal and work to resolve the situation. I've heard of too many stories where people allowed resentment to fester for years. Don't let that happen. "But I say to you that everyone who is angry with his brother will be liable to judgment; whoever insults his brother will be liable to the council; and whoever says, 'You fool!' will be liable to the hell of fire. So if you are offering your gift at the altar and there remember that your brother has something against you, leave your gift there before the altar and go. First be reconciled to your brother, and then come and offer your gift" (Matthew 5:22–24).

➤ Confess Your Part: If you have done something to cause a rift, then step up and accept responsibility. Ask God to give you the humility you need to make things right. If it means offering an apology, then the two words "I'm sorry" are worth more than ten years of separation.

➤ Tackle the Problem: An issue cannot be dealt with if it's not revealed. Be open to an honest discussion, and get to the bottom of the issue. This will lead to healing and restoration. "The wise of heart is called discerning, and sweetness of speech increases persuasiveness" (Proverbs 16:21).

➤ Mend the Fence: Put the ordeal behind you and strive to never repeat the same mistake again in the future. Most of the time, the issues that cause a wedge between people start out small and fester and grow. There are times when the situation is too big for you and me, but your problems are never too big for God. Ask the Lord for a solution, and work together to build a new fence.

Political bickering led to one of the most intense rivalries in college football. Although fans appreciate and look forward to each Auburn-Alabama football game, they should keep the contest in perspective. It's a game. You should also keep your life in perspective, and never allow the devil to drive a wedge between you and others.

DAY 4
RUN THE LENGTH OF THE FIELD

November 30, 2013: Auburn 34, Alabama 28

Delight yourself in the Lord and he will give you the desires of your heart. Commit your way to the Lord; trust in him, and he will act. He will bring forth your righteousness as the light, and your justice as the noonday. —Psalm 37:4–6

Kick Six: the play that is perhaps the greatest in the history of Auburn football.

The seventy-eighth Iron Bowl had lived up to the hype.

Number-one and undefeated Alabama was in a dogfight with Auburn, whose record stood at 10–1. A trip to the Southeastern Conference title game was at stake.

The contest was a heavyweight boxing match as both teams traded scores throughout.

For those who attended or watched on television, the game appeared to be headed into overtime with a 28–28 score and thirty-two seconds left to play.

Alabama running back T. J. Yeldon bolted through the line and ran out of bounds with the ball at the Auburn thirty-two-yard line as time expired.

But coach Nick Saban challenged the ruling and claimed his runner went out of bounds with time left.

He was right, and officials put one second back on the clock.

The Tide lined up for a fifty-seven-yard field goal to win the game and secure a berth in the SEC Championship game.

The ball was kicked and sailed through the air and looked as though it might make the target.

But Auburn's Chris Davis positioned himself in front of the goalpost in anticipation the attempt might be short.

He made the right decision and caught the kick just shy of the target deep in the end zone.

Davis had one thing on his mind. A score. No time was left, and he went all out.

He streaked past the Alabama bench while Saban and his team watched in stunned disbelief as the punt returner ran 109 yards for the score and the Auburn win.

Many sportswriters described the play as one of the greatest moments in college football history.

> The LORD is my strength and my shield; in him my heart trusts, and I am helped; my heart exults, and with my song I give thanks to him. —Psalm 28:7

WAR EAGLE

The Christian life is never dull, and there are many highs and lows you will experience. You might enjoy the wonderful news that a loved one gave their heart to the Lord, and the next day you may receive a disturbing call from your doctor with bad news. Just because you live for God does not mean you are exempt from problems.

RIDE FOR THE BRAND

You may face a similar challenge to Auburn with your back up against the goalposts. Alabama made an attempt to win the game by going for the field goal, but Chris Davis put himself in the proper position to catch the short kick. After he caught the ball, he weaved in and out and avoided tacklers to go the distance and win the game. Here are some suggestions you may consider when your back is up against the wall:

➤ Look Back on How Good God Has Been to You: Sometimes it's important to remember how the Lord has protected and helped you along the way. Reflect back on the times He came through for you at the right moment or answered your prayers even when you thought the clock had run out. This will give you the confidence you need to get through your struggles.

➤ Read His Promises to You Again: Reminders are always helpful. You set them on your phone and write them down on your calendar because you don't want to miss an important event. Take the time to read what God has told you through His written Word. Like Abraham, you can be "fully convinced that God was able to do what he had promised" (Romans 4:21).

➤ Gain Strength in Numbers: Ask a few trusted friends to pray for you and your situation. You don't have to go into detail or disclose everything you are going through. But it will help you sustain the attacks and bring you comfort when you know how many people are on your side. Davis could not have gone the distance with the ball without the other ten players on the field. He looked to them to help him make the magnificent run. He received the credit, but all played a big part. Make sure you give God the praise He deserves.

➤ See the Goal in Sight: Davis may not have seen the end zone on the other side of the field until he was about halfway there. He was probably focused on the immediate task of weaving his way through the eleven Alabama players. But once he made it to midfield, he knew he had a chance to score. The same goes for you. Obstacles and challenges might hinder your vision at first, but when you avoid the devil's tackles and high step the traps, you will see the end in sight. Don't become discouraged about the distance that remains, but instead draw inspiration from the fact that you will score the winning touchdown.

➤ Trust Your Blocker: The Christian journey is not easy. You will get hit hard along the way and thrown for a loss now and then. But this doesn't mean you will lose. The Iron Bowl initially looked like it was going to go into overtime. Then the potential outcome shifted to a Bama win. But Davis was ready to field the ball and go the distance. He trusted his team to help him cross the goal line after he ran 109 yards. Your situation might look promising and then suddenly appear to be hopeless. That's when you need to put yourself in position and allow God to lead you down the field. "And we know for those who love God all things work together for good, for those who are called according to his purpose" (Romans 8:28).

Chris Davis knew if he caught the ball shy of the goalposts, he had a chance to return the kick and go the distance. The odds were not in his favor, but he tried anyway. He demonstrated the will to win and did not give up, capitalizing on a golden opportunity. He knew he had one shot to score and win. You can have the same attitude and put yourself in a position to avoid the onslaught from the devil and go the distance with the pigskin and pull off a stunner.

DAY 5
BE LINED UP FOR THE KICK

September 18, 2010: Auburn 27, Clemson 24

Also I heard the voice of the Lord, saying, Whom shall
I send, and who will go for us? Then said I, Here am I;
send me. —Isaiah 6:8 KJV

Clemson took the opening drive and marched seventy-six yards
in a dozen plays to grab a 7–0 lead over number-sixteen ranked
Auburn at Jordan-Hare Stadium.

A field goal made it 10–0, and a sixty-one-yard five-play
drive boosted the lead to 17–0.

Auburn was able to put three points on the board before
the break when Wes Byrum nailed a thirty-five-yard field goal.

But the tide began to turn for the Tigers halfway through the
third quarter when they put together a sixty-one-yard, six-play
drive that ended with running back Onterio McCalebb's
twelve-yard run into the end zone. The drive featured a big play
when quarterback Cam Newton connected with Darvin Adams
for a thirty-four-yard strike on a third-and-one play that took
the ball inside the red zone. They later tied the game at 17–17
with a touchdown snag by Adams, who finished the game with
118 yards receiving.

Newton turned in a solid game and completed seven passes
for 203 yards with a pair of touchdowns, including a seventy-
eight-yard strike to Terrell Zachery in the third quarter to give

Auburn its first lead at 24–17. He also added sixty-eight yards on the ground.

After being dominated for nearly thirty minutes by Clemson, they whipped off twenty-four straight points.

Clemson rallied to tie the game and send it into overtime.

Byrum lined up a thirty-nine-yard field goal and sent it through the uprights to take the 27–24 lead in the extra period.

Clemson had a chance to tie the game, and in fact, did for a few seconds. Kicker Chandler Catanzaro connected on a chip shot, but it was negated when the team committed an offensive penalty. The second try missed, and Auburn held on for the overtime win.

Auburn's kick was good because Byrum stayed focused on the task at hand and made sure his attempt was lined up in the right direction. Are you lined up to boot the kick through the goal posts?

I delight to do thy will, O my God: yea, thy law is within my heart. —Psalm 40:8 KJV

WAR EAGLE

Do you find it tough to stay focused on God when the game of life goes into overtime? Everyday situations can leave you stressed and take your focus off the Lord if you are not careful. The devil will plant traps and distractions in your way to entice you to forget about your relationship with the Lord. You might have to work late on the night you promised your kids you'd be home early. Or maybe you had plans with your spouse, but a friend sent word that he desperately needs to talk. Or maybe a group of friends asks you to go to a place where you know you will be tempted to sin. Maybe you have some extra time to look at your computer. Are you lined up in the right direction? Are you doing the things that will help keep you on the straight and narrow?

RIDE FOR THE BRAND

In order for a place kicker to be successful, he must spend hours in practice and imagine himself in the game. His focus must be laser-like, and his concentration must be at an all-time high. He cannot let distractions come into play, or he will run the risk of missing the kick. Here is a list of suggestions for you to sharpen your focus on the Lord:

➤ Plan Quiet Time with God: This will not happen without you making it a priority. Set aside time each day, whether it's when you first wake up or before you turn in for the night. Make a daily appointment with Christ, and don't postpone the meeting. Life is busy, but it's not too hectic for you to carve out a few minutes each day to spend with the One who created you.

➤ Make a To-Do List: I have to make one each day to accomplish anything. There is some slight satisfaction when I am able to cross off each one throughout the day. You can include items like sending an encouraging note to a friend, visiting someone in the hospital, or committing to a random act of kindness each day.

➤ Limit Your Distractions: Put your phone away while you conduct your devotions, and don't look at it during family time or at dinner. Social media can wait while you spend time with your loved ones, and you need to give them your full attention. Distractions such as your phone can keep you from hearing from God at certain times. When you put aside your electronic devices for a while, it will reduce your stress levels and allow you to focus on what is important in your life. Phones are important but not essential. Make a decision to turn off your phone for the weekend and spend time with your spouse and the Lord.

➢ Commit to Memorize a Verse of Scripture Each Month: This will take some time, but it will strengthen your spirit and allow you to fight the forces of evil when they come against you. Try to learn Scripture passages that hold meaning for you on a personal level and give you peace and comfort.

➢ Commit to Help Someone Each Week: This can be anonymous and easy. Pay for the coffee or the meal of a person in line behind you. Or you can volunteer your time to a charity. A random act of kindness will benefit everyone involved. When you give your time, you increase your focus on doing what is right. "Not with eyeservice, as menpleasers; but as servants of Christ, doing the will of God from the heart" (Ephesians 6:6 KJV).

Byrum spent years practicing for the moment when he sent the ball through the uprights to win the game. It didn't just happen. He practiced long at his craft, and it paid off in a few seconds. You can do the same. Invest time with God and His plan so you can be a winner at the end of the game of life.

DAY 6
RUN ALL OVER THE ENEMY

October 23, 2010: Auburn 24, LSU 17

But I do not account my life of any value nor as precious to myself, if only I may finish my course and the ministry that I received from the Lord Jesus, to testify to the gospel of the grace of God. —Acts 20:24

Auburn quarterback Cam Newton put on a show.

He ran all over the Louisiana State University defense for 217 yards and two touchdowns, while the team posted 440 yards on the ground.

Newton toted the pigskin twenty-eight times while running back Michael Dyer ran it fifteen times for one hundred yards as the Tiger offense ran over LSU for 526 yards in the 24–17 win.

With more than six minutes to play in the final quarter and the game tied 17–17, Auburn had the ball at its own ten-yard line.

It took them just three plays to go ninety yards.

Newton dashed up in the middle for sixteen yards, and Dyer scampered around the corner for a small gain. That's when Onterio McCalebb broke through and romped seventy yards for the go-ahead and game-winning touchdown with five minutes and five seconds to play.

Auburn scored on its second possession of the game when Newton went into the end zone for his twenty-sixth touchdown of the season, tying Pat Sullivan's single season mark.

LSU countered and closed the gap 7–3 when Josh Jasper connected on a 48-yard field goal.

Wes Byrum's kick increased the Auburn lead to 10–3, and he became the school's all-time leading scorer with 313 points.

Right before the half, LSU, which entered the game ranked sixth in the nation, tied the game when Jordan Jefferson ran seventy-eight yards for a touchdown.

Fifth-ranked Auburn took the second half kickoff and went ninety-one yards in three plays, which culminated in Newton's forty-nine-yard dash into the end zone.

The game was tied again at 17–17 when Reuben Randle caught a 39-yard touchdown pass from running back Spencer Ware.

They set the stage for McCallebb's run.

For the game, Auburn dominated the run attack and executed the strategy all the way for the win. How is your ground game?

> Do you not know that in a race all the runners run, but only one receives the prize? So run that you may obtain it. Every athlete exercises self-control in all things. They do it to receive a perishable wreath, but we an imperishable. —1 Corinthians 9:24–25

WAR EAGLE

The Christian race is similar to the great performance from Cam Newton and the offensive line. At the end of the season,

Day 6: Run All Over the Enemy

Newton took home the prestigious Heisman Trophy award for the most outstanding player in college football and led his team to the National Championship. Both accomplishments are milestones that are not easy to achieve. Your journey in faith can be compared to a marathon. It takes discipline and courage to reach the goal. You must be in shape spiritually and prepared for a defensive attack. Are you ready?

RIDE FOR THE BRAND

College football teams like Auburn have a limited number of games each year and a week to prepare for each contest. On the other hand, you face your enemy each day all year long. Your game plan must be simple and easy to understand. You don't need trick plays or razzle-dazzle formations. You must run hard to win the game and let the Lord be your lead blocker. The race needs determination and focus. Here are some suggestions on how to develop a successful game plan:

➢ Go the Entire Distance: This might seem obvious, but you won't win unless you cross the goal line. Finish what you set out to do, and plunge into the end zone.

➢ Be Disciplined: Cam Newton and the team worked out each day and were physically ready for each game. Make sure you hold daily devotions, spend time in prayer, and attend church on a regular basis. This will make you ready to take on any opponent. "But I discipline my body and keep it under control, lest after preaching to others I myself should be disqualified" (1 Corinthians 9:27).

➢ Be an Active Member of the Team: Don't hang out with people who are negative and might deter you in your Christian walk. If this is the case, find new friends and join a team of players who are positive and encourage you to do the right thing.

➢ Move the Chains: Stay away from activities or things that drag you down. For example, if Christ delivered you from alcohol, stay away from that temptation. If you were addicted to drugs, then remove those obstacles and make God your new high. Ask the Master to open new doors for you and shut the old ones.

➢ Focus on the Goal Line: When you run the race, always envision the goal line in your mind. There might be times when it's difficult to see, especially if you are in a valley, but have the mindset to know it's there. Look forward to the wonderful prize that awaits you. Cam Newton and the Auburn Tigers had a goal to win the National Championship. There were moments throughout the season when they might have doubted, but it was only for a brief time. When you are a believer in the Lord, your prize will be a robe and crown and a home in heaven. "Set your mind on the things that are above, not on things that are on earth" (Colossians 3:2).

Sometimes the defense comes through the line and sacks you for a loss. But don't become discouraged. Regroup in the huddle and call the right play. Let the Lord block for you and scamper down the field for the game-winning touchdown run. Be determined to run the race to win. When the season ends, you will know you are on the winning side and will receive the ultimate prize.

DAY 7
ROLL OVER THE DEVIL

January 10, 2011: Auburn 22, Oregon 19

Man shall not live by bread alone, but by every word
that proceeds from the mouth of God. —Matthew 4:4
NKJV

Several athletes throughout history have special moments from
their careers that are forever remembered in time and link
them to greatness.

New York Yankees fans will always have "the flip" from
Derek Jeter. The Boston Celtics overcame adversity when
Larry Bird "stole the ball." And the history of the San Francisco
49ers includes "the catch" from Dwight Clark.

All were defining moments in a career.

Auburn's Michael Dyer will always be remembered when
he "rolled over" the Ducks.

The National Championship game was tied 19–19, and the
Tigers had the ball for the final time.

Cam Newton led his squad, ranked number one and 13–0,
down the field on a quest to win the school's first title since
1957.

But Dyer was the one who made the incredible play that
stunned everyone, even himself.

The running back appeared to be stopped in his tracks by Oregon's Eddie Pleasant, who trapped him for what looked like a gain of only seven yards.

The two went to the ground, but Dyer landed on top of Pleasant and used the defender's body as a shield between him and the ground. He rolled over without his knees ever touching the ground.

He was able to get his feet under him and took off for a gain of thirty-seven yards, taking the ball to the Oregon twenty-three-yard line with a few seconds to go.

His dynamic play set the tone for the dramatic win when Wes Byrum connected on a nineteen-yard field goal as time expired and gave Auburn the National Championship.

Dyer finished the game with 143 yards on 22 carries, while Newton racked up 265 yards in the air and completed 20 of 34 passing attempts and two touchdowns.

When the day was over, the Auburn Tigers football team was the king of the college football world.

But it took a magnificent play and the will to succeed from Dyer.

Will you roll over the enemy?

The LORD is my rock and my fortress and my deliverer; my God, my strength, in whom will I trust; my shield and the horn of my salvation, my stronghold. —Psalm 18:2 NKJV

Day 7: Roll Over the Devil

WAR EAGLE

There might be times when the devil has you in his grasp, and it might look as though you are going down to the turf. You envisioned a touchdown, but all of a sudden you find yourself being tackled. You go to the ground and land on top of the defender. Your knees don't touch, which means you are still allowed to run. Will you have the presence of mind to know you are still in the game and continue? Or will you give up and accept being thrown for a loss? The devil wants to take you down and keep you from scoring, and he will toss obstacles in your way to impede your progression. His goal is to attempt to catch you off guard and find ways to bring discouragement. But it's time to roll over.

RIDE FOR THE BRAND

Everyone faces challenges in life. You might be faced with a job loss or an illness you didn't see coming. You could be blind-sided by a relationship struggle or be the focal point of a lie on social media. No matter the circumstance, you can realize your knee is not on the turf, and you can continue on your Christian journey. The devil might have hold of you, but he did not take you all the way down to the ground. Here are some ways you can get up and roll over to fight for victory:

> Roll Over in Praise: Solid and strong Christians find their strength by giving praise and honor to the Lord. They don't do it to ensure good things will happen; they praise God because He is worthy, and they know He will give them hope and peace through times of trial. You might

33

feel Satan's grip, but through praise you will find the strength to roll over the enemy and keep running. "I will bless the LORD at all times; his praise shall continually be in my mouth" (Psalm 34:1 NKJV).

➤ Roll Over in Prayer: There is never a problem too small to talk to God about, and He will hear you in all times and all situations. People tend to spend more time in prayer when the Lord's presence is needed in a desperate hour, and this is understandable. But you should try to make it a point to talk to the Heavenly Father as often as you can throughout the day. He longs to hear from you. Always take the time to thank Him for His blessings before you give Him your requests. When you have regular conversation with God, you will find the power to roll over and keep running.

➤ Roll Over Negative Baggage: The devil will try to bring up your past to bring you down. You may have lived a rough lifestyle, but you can put those days behind you. Don't allow the forces of evil to drag you down in the gutter with thoughts from years gone by. Christ died for your sins, and once you repent and ask for His forgiveness, He tosses them into the sea of forgetfulness. Refuse to carry heavy weight around with you. Michael Dyer could not have pulled off the thirty-seven-yard run if he was dragging a twenty-five-pound bag of sand behind him. "Therefore we also, since we are surrounded by so great a cloud of witnesses, let us lay aside every weight, and the sin which so easily ensnares us, and let us run with endurance the race that is set before us" (Hebrews 12:1 NKJV).

➤ Roll Over in Fellowship: When you surround yourself with like-minded people who have the same desire to serve God as you do, you will find encouragement to keep going. Your friends and loved ones also go through tense situations, but there is comfort in numbers. Make sure you attend church and Sunday school or a Bible study on a regular basis. Become involved in extracurricular activities offered through your church or help out with a charity. Your teammates will lift you up and cheer you on as you roll over the enemy.

➤ Roll Over in Testimony: Show the love of God to others through your speech and daily actions. You may be the only Bible some people will ever read, so make an effort to always be a witness for Christ. Ask God to give you opportunities to share your faith, and when He opens those doors, ask Him to help put the right words in your mouth. Be sure your friends, family, and coworkers know you have a testimony. Memorize verses of Scripture you can use to maintain your witness in the face of a trial, and ask your Master for grace to help you find the strength to get up and roll over. "Death and life are in the power of the tongue" (Proverbs 18:21 NKJV).

Dyer's play epitomized determination and the will to win. He did not let the defender take him all the way to the ground. He rolled over and set up his team for the game-winner. When you are determined to succeed in your own Christian journey, you will be able to roll over in the tough times.

DAY 8
RUN THROUGH THE STORM

December 3, 1983: Auburn 23, Alabama 20

He made the storm be still, and the waves of the sea were hushed. —Psalm 107:29

Severe weather was expected and predicted for 1983's Iron Bowl.

Some local forecasters said a supercell could produce tornadic activity, and strong storms were possible

But this was the Iron Bowl—college football's biggest rivalry. No tornado would keep fans away from Legion Field in Birmingham, Alabama.

The weather was pleasant at the start of the game. But as the event went on, dark clouds rolled in and covered the field.

Fans knew something was up when the Goodyear blimp flew away before the start of the third quarter. This was a bad sign that strong storms were on the way.

With about three minutes left on the clock in the third quarter, Auburn had a 16–14 lead. Alabama's Ricky Moore dashed fifty-seven yards for a touchdown, and the Tide rolled to a 20–16 advantage.

But the Tigers answered when running-back sensation Bo Jackson ripped through the Bama defense and rumbled seventy-one yards for the go-ahead and eventual game-winning touchdown.

Jackson ran all over the Alabama defense and compiled 256 yards rushing in only 20 carries for an average of 12.8 yards per tote.

The performance was the second-best yard-per-rush in Southeastern Conference history.

After Auburn took the lead, the storms rolled in, the wind blew hard, and the weather was fierce.

The public address announcer read warnings over the speakers, but play continued.

Rain pelted the players and fans, but the contest went on in lousy conditions. The game was being televised on ABC, but viewers could barely make out what was going on because of the downpour.

Seven tornados ravaged Alabama that day, but none came close to the game's location. Auburn hung on and won the game 23–20.

The Tigers withstood the terrible storm and came out the winner. What storms have you encountered? Did you take shelter? Were you able to break through the line and run for a touchdown?

The LORD is good, a stronghold in the day of trouble;
he knows those who take refuge in him. —Nahum 1:7

WAR EAGLE

You might be going through a severe personal storm. Your situation might start out sunny, then dark clouds quickly roll in and threaten your future. Your friends may see the signs and leave, just like the blimp did when the pilots saw the horizon. The winds may howl, and the rain might come down in buckets and hinder your vision. When the Iron Bowl storm ended, three people were dead as a result of the tornados across the state. You might be facing difficult times and feel unprotected from the storms of life. But take comfort and know that they won't last forever. Trust God to make the dark clouds give way to sunshine, and you will be able to burst through the line and sprint your way to the goal line.

RIDE FOR THE BRAND

Everyone faces challenges and storms. Some might appear severe at times, while others could be considered a light shower. In either case, there are ways to make it through the storm to see a brighter day. Here are some things to remember when going through a trial.

➢ Know the One Who Calms the Storm: You can either sink or swim. When you have a personal relationship with the Master, ask God for deliverance, and your chances of surviving to see another day will increase. Lift your eyes, and focus on the Lord and His plans for you. He will not let you drown in the storm. "And he awoke and rebuked the wind and said to the sea, 'Peace! Be still!' And the wind ceased, and there was a great calm. He said

to them, 'Why are you so afraid? Have you still no faith?'"
(Mark 4:39–40).

➤ God Will Show Up Just in Time: He comes through
in the clutch. Bo Jackson whipped off a huge run at
the right moment to lift Auburn to the win. Christ, in
turn, can do the same for you. At times, you may feel as
though He has forgotten you, but you have to trust that
His timing is perfect. Don't get ahead of His plan; ask
Him for strength and courage while you wait. "Do not
fear or be in dread of them, for it is the LORD your God
who goes with you. He will not leave you or forsake you"
(Deuteronomy 31:6).

➤ Don't Focus on the Storm: When you are surrounded by
bad weather, you must look up to the Lord for direction.
Focus on things you can control, like your prayer life and
time spent in the Word. Let go, turn turn your problems
over to God, and watch Him blow the clouds away.

➤ Strengthen Your Faith: Your patience and determination
will grow stronger during this time of trial. When you
fall on your knees and lift your arms in praise, your faith
and reliance on Christ will grow. This doesn't mean you
should avoid your circumstances and do nothing, but be
sure to pay attention to God as He makes the calls from
the booth. Watch and wait. "Not only that, but we rejoice
in our sufferings, knowing that suffering produced
endurance" (Romans 5:3).

Day 8: Run through the Storm

➤ Be Willing to Get Rained On: Auburn had to play through the downpour in order to win. God never promised sunny skies with 72 degrees every day of your life. You will go through storms, but God will always be there to dry you off and point you to victory. You might have to endure situations you never dreamed possible. Illness might come to your family or you could deal with financial issues. Allow the Lord to provide you with an umbrella and a promise of better days ahead.

Bo Jackson tromped through the rain for his team, and he turned in a magnificent performance that day under difficult circumstances. He could have used the weather as an excuse to quit, but he chose to excel under challenging conditions. You can do the same. Lift your arms in praise, and allow the Holy Spirit to lead you through the storms of life and come out a winner.

DAY 9
KICK YOUR WAY THROUGH LIFE'S DISAPPOINTMENTS

January 1, 1984: Auburn 9, Michigan 7

And after you have suffered a little while, the God of all grace, who has called you to his eternal glory in Christ, will himself restore, confirm, strengthen, and establish you. —1 Peter 5:10

Auburn entered the 1984 Sugar Bowl ranked third in the nation and faced the eighth-ranked Michigan Wolverines.

Earlier in the day, Nebraska was at the number-one spot while Texas was ranked number two.

But the unexpected happened when both top-ranked teams lost that day. Georgia defeated the Longhorns of Texas while Miami upset the Cornhuskers.

By all logical calculations, if Auburn won the game, they would win the National Championship.

The Wolverines got on the board in the first quarter when quarterback Steve Smith ran in from four yards out. They held the 7–0 lead going into the halftime break.

Auburn's offense pushed the Michigan defense and ran the ball throughout the game. Bo Jackson led the way with 131

43

yards on the ground. Overall, the team produced 301 yards rushing.

Halfway through the third quarter, Tigers kicker Al Del Greco booted a thirty-one-yard field goal to cut the lead to 7–3.

A thirty-two-yarder from Del Greco in the final period trimmed Michigan's lead to 7–6.

Michigan tried to answer, but Auburn's Gregg Carr picked off a pass, which set up a drive that took the ball to the Wolverine two-yard line.

The stage was set for Del Greco to win the game and kick the Tigers to a National Championship.

His nineteen-yard field goal was good, and Auburn won the game 9–7. Del Greco accounted for all of the team's points, and a big celebration took place. The team had achieved the biggest accomplishment in college football.

But the next morning, Auburn found out that Miami, who had knocked off Nebraska, jumped them in the polls and took over the number-one spot.

The Cornhuskers, who had just been defeated, fell one spot to number two.

Auburn, who had beaten Michigan, remained number three while the Hurricanes were awarded the National Championship.

Fans were outraged and confused while players and coaches were stunned.

The players did all they could to win the crown, but officials decided to give it to another team.

Just like that.

Day 9: Kick Your Way through Life's Disappointments

Have you ever been so disappointed in life that it made you want to give up? How did you handle the situation?

> Let not your heart envy sinners, but continue in the fear of the LORD all the day. Surely there is a future, and your hope will not be cut off. —Proverbs 23:17–18

WAR EAGLE

If you are like most people, you have faced disappointments. And chances are you will encounter more before your journey is over. It's called life. You might follow the rules, but not everyone else does. There will be moments when outcomes will not appear to be fair, but you must address them and deal with them. You may get overlooked for a promotion at work or miss out on the final round of job interviews. You might be cruising along life at an enjoyable pace when you are suddenly blindsided by an accident accompanied by health issues. That vacation of a lifetime might have to be put on hold because of unexpected financial issues. Just like that.

RIDE FOR THE BRAND

When bad luck comes your way, it's easy to feel outraged and angry and lash out at your friends and family. People oftentimes take out their frustrations on those who love them the most. No matter if someone chooses another team over you, there are ways to handle your disappointments in life. Here are some suggestions for how to appreciate your own victories:

➤ It's Okay to Question God: You can ask Him why if that makes you feel better. We all try to understand why bad things happen to "good" people, and there are often no obvious reasons. It's human nature to wonder why. Why do people die in war? Why do children become ill? Why? We may never know the answers until we reach heaven. Ask God to give you peace and help you trust His plan.

➤ Accept the Outcome: Sooner or later, you will have to accept what took place. Auburn fans felt robbed of the championship, but they still showed up to attend games the next year to cheer on their Tigers. Never sulk or allow bitterness to take over your personality. You don't have to like the outcome, but you must face reality and move on to the next phase of your life.

➤ Don't Hold Grudges: Grudges only invite the devil to bring bitterness into your heart. If you think you deserved a promotion more than the coworker who received it, do not make yourself miserable by holding a grudge. Instead, congratulate them and offer your assistance to help in the future. Be an adult, and be happy for the person. Even though Auburn fans felt they deserved the number-one spot over Miami, their lives went on the next day, and the world did not end. "Be angry and do not sin; do not let the sun go down on your anger" (Ephesians 4:26).

➤ Move On: After you have come to terms with what has transpired, make the decision to move on with your life. If you feel you have been wronged, hold you head up high, put your ego behind you, and continue with your life and plans for your future. A temporary setback will not keep you from the end zone.

➢ Expect to Win the Next Game: Auburn entered the Sugar Bowl with expectations of winning. They were behind in the first quarter but did not give up. Al Del Greco produced and booted his team to victory. Enter each day with the knowledge and confidence that you are on the winning team.

Auburn did all it could to win the National Championship, but it was not meant to be. The two teams in front of them lost, while they pulled out the win. By any other standard, Auburn should have been selected the best team in college football. But for some reason, Miami was tapped. When life does not seem fair, get back up and go to work to put yourself in position to claim the title the next time.

DAY 10
KEEP THE PACE AND THE FAITH

December 7, 2013: Auburn 59, Missouri 42

I have chosen the way of truth: thy judgments have I laid before me. —Psalm 119:30 KJV

The 2013 Southeastern Conference Championship Game would have been perfect for the Fourth of July.

Both Tiger squads lit up the scoreboard with offensive productions and fireworks.

Missouri put three points on the board in the first quarter on a field goal, but Auburn answered with a thirty-eight-yard touchdown strike from Nick Marshall to Sammie Coates for the 7–3 lead.

The Mizzou offense rallied, and Dorial Green-Beckham hauled in a twenty-eight-yard pass and jumped in front 10–7. The ball was dropped, but Auburn did not challenge the result of the play.

It was Auburn's turn to score, and Marshall answered the call with a nine-yard scamper.

Missouri's defense stepped up and stripped Marshall of the ball on Auburn's next possession and took it to the house for a 17–14 lead.

Once again, Auburn responded when Tre Mason scored on a seven-yard run and took the 21–17 lead. After a Missouri field goal, Mason scored again to boost their advantage to 28–20.

The score at the break was 28–27 after Missouri scored a touchdown to keep the pace with Auburn. Fans loved the high-scoring performances.

Auburn fell behind 34–31 in the third but slowly took over the contest and wore down Missouri.

They went on a 28–8 run and scored at will as the defense could not keep up with the furious offensive production.

Marshall darted forty-two yards and set up an eight-yard scoring run by Corey Grant, and the onslaught was in full force.

Auburn ran for 536 yards on the ground, which established an SEC title game record.

Missouri could not keep up with the Auburn offense and ran out of steam. They could not keep the pace.

The win set the stage for Auburn to play for the national title a month later.

Have you ever run out of gas like Mizzou did? Are you able to pour it on for the Lord like Auburn?

Jesus said unto him, if thou canst believe, all things are possible to him that believeth. —Mark 9:23 KJV

WAR EAGLE

Life, just like the SEC title game against Auburn and Missouri, can be fast-paced and high-scoring. You try to hold down a job, raise a family, and serve as a mentor to those who look to you for guidance. There never seems to be a time when you can power down and relax. In all the hustle and bustle of your daily journey, you may find it hard to stay focused on what matters the most—your relationship with Christ. Do you become overwhelmed at times and fall behind? Are you able to keep the pace and the faith with the Lord?

RIDE FOR THE BRAND

The Master is faithful to you, and you should always strive to be faithful to Him. This is often complicated by human nature and the weakness of the flesh combined with selfish stubbornness and self-indulgence, but you can do it with His help. Winning an SEC title is not easy, and neither is living a dedicated life for Jesus. But here are some suggestions to make it possible:

➢ Be Strong-Willed: There will be challenging situations in your life, and you must lean on God through those times. You must demonstrate an unwavering trust in the Lord to take care of you. Dive into the Word of God every day. Auburn's offensive players could not pull off the performance had they not known the playbook inside and out. The Bible is your guide each day for winning. "Therefore, my beloved brethren, be ye steadfast, unmovable, always abounding in the work of the Lord, forasmuch as ye know that your labour is not in vain in the Lord" (1 Corinthians 15:58 KJV).

➢ Don't Be Distracted by the World: This step is not as easy as it may sound. If you are a child of God, you enjoy the thoughts of heaven and the Father. But it's also easy to become caught up in the ways of the world too. You are bombarded with advertisements and attractions from the world that can easily derail you. Do not set your sights on the things of this world but set them on your reward when your journey is completed. You are fine to take part in activities such as your child's football games or festivities. But make sure you don't get so caught up that you lose focus on what is important. Associate with like-minded believers and walk together. Auburn played as a team to defeat Missouri, and you need Christian fellowship to win life's race. "Be ye not unequally yoked together with unbelievers; for what fellowship hath righteousness with unrighteousness? And what communion hath light with darkness?" (2 Corinthians 6:14 KJV).

➢ Do What's Right: There will be moments when you might have to choose between right and wrong. These are tests you must pass. When you are a Christian, your character will come into play and your integrity will be at stake. You might be put in a situation where a "little white lie" might be the best way out of a sticky predicament. Do what is right and just in the eyes of the Lord, even if it leads to negative consequences. Sin is never worth the cost.

➢ Be Obedient: Football players must follow rules and instructions from the coaches. If not, they might collect penalties or even be removed from the game or the team. The same goes for you. The Lord will give you direction, and you must take it if you want to succeed. Sometimes,

Day 10: Keep the Pace and the Faith

you might not understand, but you must trust His coaching.

➤ Show Love Toward Others: The Lord will honor you if you treat others with love and respect. He will not bless you if you walk over people to get to the top. Be humble, and serve others each day, walking "with all lowliness and meekness, with longsuffering, forbearing one another in love" (Ephesians 4:2 KJV).

Auburn ran wild in the SEC title game and outlasted Missouri. They wore down their opponent and went on to claim the conference banner. Mizzou could not keep the pace and lost the battle. Be determined to stay focused on God's will for your life, and your ability to keep the faith and win the title will increase.

DAY 11
STAY FOCUSED ON GOD

December 3, 1949: Auburn 14, Alabama 13

Set your mind on things that are above, not on things
that are on earth. —Colossians 3:2

The season before, Alabama thumped Auburn 55–0.

And the 1949 season wasn't going well either.

The Tigers entered the game at Legion Field in Birmingham
with a 1–4–3 record while the Tide rolled in with a 6–2–1 mark.

Bama fans and players were confident they would win
another Iron Bowl.

But the Tigers scored first when Johnny Wallis picked off a
Crimson Tide pass and returned it for a score.

Alabama answered and tied the game 7–7 just before the half.

Everyone already knew this was not going to be a repeat of
the previous rout. Auburn came to play.

Early in the fourth quarter, Auburn drove seventy-one
yards for a touchdown and took a 14–7 lead.

The Tide came back and put together a fifty-one-yard drive
that ended in a touchdown. The game would be tied after the
extra-point kick.

Auburn lined up to defend the PAT and drew the attention of
kicker Eddie Salem, who anticipated a rush and missed the boot.

He lost his concentration and focused on the defense instead of on the task at hand.

Auburn ran out the clock and took the victory from a stunned Alabama team and fans.

The Tiger faithful did not want to leave the arena and celebrated long after the game ended.

Many had rented cushions packed with feathers, and they began to rip them apart until much of the field was covered in feathers.

What a difference a year can make.

Do you keep your eyes on the Lord? Or are you distracted by the defense?

Let your eyes look directly forward, and your gaze be straight before you. —Proverbs 4:25

WAR EAGLE

You might have suffered a disappointing defeat in the past and may have reservations about facing the opponent once again. You might be distracted by something that happened weeks before that left a bad taste in your mouth. Perhaps a loved one or someone you trusted let you down. Everyone will lose a battle throughout life, but how you respond is what matters. You cannot keep your eyes fixed on the past. You must depend on God to lead you into the field and compete to win.

RIDE FOR THE BRAND

When memories of the past make you afraid to face your future, you must meet your fears head on and overcome them with God's help. Only He can lead the charge for you to deliver the upset win. Here are some ways to stay focused on God's game plan for you:

➤ Get Self Out of the Way: Getting out of the way is the first step. Kick your ego through the uprights or leave it in the locker room. When disappointments come, you may try to take control of the situation and come up with your own answers. But God's plan is always better, and He will never fail you when you give Him the reins. You may have plans and aspirations, but you also need to know when to surrender to His master plan. "Oh, the depth of the riches and wisdom and knowledge of God! How unsearchable are his judgments and how inscrutable his ways!" (Romans 11:33).

➤ Flee from Bad Influences: If there is something or someone that pulls you away from spending time with the Lord, then it must be addressed. A friend will not ask you to miss church or make fun of you for praying and reading your Bible. Enjoying time on the golf course is great, but that should never come before going to the Lord's house. Pay attention when the Holy Spirit nudges you about what you are doing or who are you with. Take heed of negative influences. "Be not wise in your own eyes; fear the LORD, and turn away from evil" (Proverbs 3:7).

➤ Put God First in All Things: When something good happens to you, always remember to give God all the praise. When you trust God with your future and put Him first, He will prepare you for His way and His will, which are always better than our own plans and dreams. Make God your priority, and place your hope in His plan for your life.

➤ Listen and Obey: When children disobey their parents' instructions, they often face some form of punishment. In many cases, if they had just listened and followed directions, they may have been saved from danger or heartache. The same goes for our relationship with the Master. God knows what is best for you because He has your future in His hands. If He says no, He has a reason, and you don't always have to know why. He loves you and knows what is best for you, and He could be saving you from a potential horrible outcome that you may never know about, so accept His decisions and be excited about what He has next for you.

➤ Praise the Lord: Worship the Lord and give Him praise during the ups and downs. He will prepare you for each game and for every practice. You might have come off a big loss and feel embarrassed, as was the case when Auburn lost 55–0. Praise God anyway. Look for the blessing, and anticipate great things ahead. The Tigers came back from a staggering loss the year before and defeated Alabama. Always remember where God has brought you from, and praise Him for the victories that lie ahead.

Alabama's kicker was distracted and missed the PAT to tie the game. The result was a win for Auburn. You cannot lose sight of God in your life. If you do, you will miss more than an extra point. Stay focused, and don't make mistakes to distract you from the hope of eternal life in heaven.

DAY 12
CARRY ON THE TRADITION

February 20, 1892: Auburn 10, Georgia 0

Be imitators of me, as I am of Christ. Now I commend you because you remember me in everything and maintain the traditions even as I delivered them to you.
—2 Thessalonians 3:6

All traditions have a beginning.

A wonderful rivalry began on this date in Atlanta when Auburn, known at that time as the Agricultural and Mechanical College of Alabama, met Georgia.

In the South, football was new and attractive to fans.

The sport was a big hit in the Ivy League schools and was embraced by a Yale University professor named Walter Camp. The recreational activity garnered attention, and the excitement spread to Georgia and Alabama. Professors from each of the schools arranged the contest, based on Camp's guidelines.

The meeting was the first of the season for Auburn and the second for Georgia.

About 3,000 people came to the game at Piedmont Park, which Auburn won 10–0. But that was not the most important thing that happened. There were two great outcomes.

Auburn Believer

The rivalry between the two teams has been dubbed the Deep South's Oldest Rivalry and has been played nearly continuously since 1892.

And it was during this inaugural rivalry game that Auburn established the battle cry of "War Eagle."

There are several versions of how the battle cry began, but the story from Auburn University is that the "War Eagle" is more of a battle cry or theme, rather than a nickname.

"When the two teams met on the turf that day, one of the fans in the stands was a veteran of the Civil War. He brought with him a pet Bald Eagle that he had kept for more than three decades since the war had ended.

As the story goes, the Eagle broke lose from his owner during the game and soared high into the air to circle the field. The majestic sight of the proud bird drew everyone's attention.

At the same time, Auburn started a drive that led to a touchdown to clinch the game.

The combination of the Eagle flying high along with the drive prompted fans to being to chant "War Eagle." Fans took it as an omen of good luck, and the term lived on to symbolize the spirt of the Auburn Tigers.

When the game ended, the Eagle dove to the ground and died.

Traditions are a fun way to bring a team or family together, and it's never too late to start one. What ones have you started or want to begin?

And what you have heard from me in the presence of many witnesses entrust to faithful men, who will be able to teach others also. —2 Timothy 2:2

WAR EAGLE

There are many scenarios for this devotional. You could be a new believer in the Lord and want to begin a cool and nifty tradition, one that will give you a solid foundation for your journey. Or you might be a new parent and have a desire to pass something down to your children. And there could be the occasion where you and your spouse are expecting a child and want to plan something unique for them as they grow older. Traditions must have a beginning, so why not now?

RIDE FOR THE BRAND

The list of traditions can be lengthy, but you should find one that fits your personality. Don't make one just for the sake of it. I know in my family, for example, we like to read the Christmas story verse by verse before we exchange gifts. We also enjoy watching selected movies as a family once a year. They are wonderful and can strengthen a relationship. Here are some suggestions on what you can do to bring a tradition in your home.

> Annual Photo Shoot: A photo shoot will show the progression of your family each year. Pick a theme and stick with it. It can be in the fall with colorful leave and haystacks, at Christmas in front of the same decorations each year, or in the spring when life blooms again.

> A Weekend Getaway: This can be done each quarter or on an annual basis. The key here is to make time for the special people in your life. It can be with your spouse, kids, or other family. If you have more than one child, take turns

taking each one for a special weekend—or even just a special day out. Let them know they are appreciated, and pour out your attention on only them. Maybe each special occasion will be to visit a different ballpark or to those fun, local attractions like the "world's biggest ball of yarn."

➤ A Time Capsule: Each year at an agreed time, have members of your family contribute one or two items to a box that is locked. They could include a picture or a note or a ticket to a cool event. After five years, open it together and relive the memories.

➤ Draw a Vacation Destination from a Hat: Have each member of the family write down where they want to go, and draw a winner. This is a great way to be unpredictable and include all in the process. You can establish criteria so that you don't end up in a bizarre place, but for the most part be lighthearted and accommodating.

➤ The Cookoff: Each quarter, pick a member of the family or a friend and have them make everyone dinner. Even if they don't cook, it can become a fun tradition, and they might learn the art of preparing food. It might be fun, and it will teach them valuable skills later in life. You can go all out for this one and even have a dress for dinner atmosphere along with a theme.

Auburn fans adore the tradition of the War Eagle, and it has become part of the team's home game experience. Make your own tradition that will last for years to come. It might be something that your grandchildren enjoy so much that they continue to hand it down from generation to generation.

DAY 13
WHAT DO YOU EXPECT?

January 2, 1971: Auburn 35, Ole Miss 28

He that loveth not knoweth not, for God is love.
—1 John 4:8 KJV

The 1971 Gator Bowl featured two high-profile quarterbacks who could put up big numbers.

Auburn's Pat Sullivan was a terrific athlete who would go on to win the Heisman Trophy and the Walter Camp Award after the 1971 season.

Archie Manning, who was under center for Ole Miss, was the Southeastern Conference Player of the Year in 1969.

Fans were in store for a gem because these teams did not meet often.

Sullivan's main target was Terry Beasley, an All-American receiver, and Alvin Bresler, who was fast as lightning.

Manning, a wizard at quarterback, had fractured his arm earlier in the season and was not playing up to his full potential. But he reached down to turn in a magnificent performance for the loss.

Auburn whipped off three straight touchdowns and grabbed a 21–0 lead thanks to connections from Sullivan to Beasley and Bresler.

The Rebels countered as Manning scampered into the end zone and later found Floyd Franks on a touchdown pass to cut the lead to 21–14 before the half.

The Tigers picked up where they left off and scored in the third quarter when Mickey Zofko crossed the end zone to increase their lead to 28–14.

Manning led charges to come back but fell short in the attempt as Auburn claimed the title with the 35–28 win.

Sullivan was a master on the field and passed for 351 yards and two touchdowns. He added a rushing touchdown and earned MVP honors.

Larry Willingham returned four punts for Auburn for ninety-three yards, a Gator Bowl record that remains on the books to this day.

The Auburn quarterback used an arsenal of weapons and kept throwing to his targets to win the game. Fortunately for his team and fans, he turned in one of the best performances in the history of the school and exceeded everyone's expectations.

Is God meeting your expectations? What do you look for God to do for you in your Christian journey?

We love him, because he first loved us. —1 John 4:19 KJV

WAR EAGLE

You might be under the misconception that the Lord owes you something once you turn your life over to Him. Perhaps you assume you will receive a long, prosperous, and healthy life free of trials and problems. Even though you faithfully attend church, read your Bible, pray every day, and live a life that pleases the Lord, you are not exempt from challenges. Do you anticipate God to bail you out of difficult situations? He might. And then again, He may have personally signed off on this test to teach you how to trust Him. What do you expect from the Master?

RIDE FOR THE BRAND

To be blunt, God does not owe you anything. On the other hand, you are in debt to His mercy and forgiveness and for His merciful gift of salvation. God is not interested in your worldly achievements and social status. He is more concerned with the way you respond to your circumstances and situations. Oftentimes, real life will not play out exactly as you had hoped, and hardships, such as job losses and health problems, may be right around the corner. Disruptions like these may bring frustration and anxiety and catch you off guard, but in the midst of your storm, remember that you can always expect the following:

> ➢ His Love Will Never Change: You may be in love with someone who you plan to spend the rest of your life with, but shifting circumstances and emotions may lead to a breakup. There will be times when relationships hurt, but the love the Father has for you will never change. You can count on this. When times get tough, you can always depend on His love for you no matter the situation. "For God so loved the world, that he gave his only begotten Son, that whosoever believeth in him should not perish, but have everlasting life" (John 3:16 KJV).

➢ You Are Always in His Presence, Even When You Can't Feel Him: There might be times in your life when you feel left out. You might have colleagues who don't invite you to lunch, or there might be times when a close group of friends gets together without you. Loneliness may be difficult to handle, and most want to feel like they belong. But know that God is always with you in the good times and the bad. When you feel alone, He is always nearby to draw close to you and bring you peace. "Teaching them to observe all things whatsoever I have commanded you: and, lo, I am with you always, even unto the end of the world. Amen" (Matthew 28:20 KJV).

➢ He Will Take Care of You: You can trust God to provide for you, even though He may not always do it in the way you envisioned. He might give you a dream job, or He might have something better in store for you. This doesn't mean you don't make plans for your future, but you must be willing to follow His plan for you too. It's okay to go to school and study a certain subject to prepare yourself for your dream career. But when things don't go your way, always know He has your best interests at heart and will not forsake you.

➢ You Are Redeemed: Once you make the decision to follow Christ, all of your sins are forgiven, and you are His child. His shed blood on the Cross has paid the price for our sins and has given us freedom and hope of eternal life. Make sure you attend His house of worship on a regular basis, find comfort in daily reading the Word of

Day 13: What Do You Expect?

God, and consistently pray to your Heavenly Father. He will pour out His blessings on you.

➤ You Have a Home in Heaven: Our heavenly mansion is the ultimate reward. You might live a prosperous life and help others financially. Or you might struggle with money and face challenges along the way. But nobody can take their earthly treasures to heaven with them. If you ask Jesus into your heart, live for Him, and follow His will, God has promised you eternal life.

Fans loved the Gator Bowl because it lived up to the hype, and they got what they expected. The game was high-scoring and featured fantastic performances from elite players. You too can expect God to take care of you, and all He wants in return is your praise and service to Him.

DAY 14
YOU CAN HAVE AN EARTH-MOVING PRAYER LIFE

October 8, 1988: LSU 7, Auburn 6

Then shall ye call upon me, and ye shall go and pray unto me, and I will hearken unto you. —Jeremiah 29:12 KJV

The game isn't remembered so much for the play on the field this day but for what happened after a touchdown.

The Southeastern Conference matchup in Louisiana pitted rivals Auburn and LSU.

Auburn was undefeated and ranked number four in the polls while LSU stood at 2–2.

Defense was the name of the game as both squads had trouble moving the ball up and down the field.

A field goal by Win Lyle gave Auburn a 3–0 lead at the half.

Another successful boot increased the lead to 6–0 with 10:18 to play in the game, and the capacity crowd of nearly eighty thousand people in Baton Rouge was ready to erupt if LSU came through.

With less than two minutes to play, LSU quarterback Tommy Hodson orchestrated a drive that ended in a touchdown when Eddie Fuller caught an eleven-yard pass on fourth down.

The reaction from the crowd was so massive as the fans roared with approval it registered as an earthquake by a seismograph at the Howe-Russell Geoscience Complex, which was located about one thousand feet from the football stadium.

The reading was discovered the next morning, and the news spread all over campus.

The response from the crowd and the outcome will forever be remembered as The Earthquake Game.

The game was a hard-fought battle, and as Christians, we also face some tough struggles against the devil and his team of angels. We need the power of God as we seek Him in prayer for strength and wisdom.

Do you have an earth-shaking prayer life? You can.

Call unto me, and I will answer thee, and show thee great and mighty things, which thou knowest not.
—Jeremiah 33:3 KJV

WAR EAGLE

The devil puts up a strong defense to keep you out of the end zone of prayer. He knows this is your best connection to the Master. If he can prevent you from talking to the Head Coach, then he has a chance to defeat you and claim the victory. He will throw in penalty distractions and use discouragement to interrupt your personal time with God. If you have kids, then you know how difficult it is to converse with them when they are on their phones or viewing social media. Satan does not play fair and knows there is power in prayer. This is why one of his main tactics is to interfere with your prayer life.

RIDE FOR THE BRAND

When you spend time in conversation with the Lord, it's your personal opportunity to talk about the plans He has for you. How would you feel if your spouse, children, or friends didn't talk to you for a few days? You might feel deserted and start looking for other people to talk to. This is what the devil wants to do with you. His game plan includes trick plays that will sack you in the backfield and entice you away from Christ. If he can obstruct the time you spend in prayer, then he hopes you might forget about your prayer life and look to him for guidance. Loneliness is a companion for darkness, and that is where he lives. Here are some ways to make sure you make the most of the time you spend with the Lord in prayer:

➢ Know Who's in the Huddle: When you pray, and you should do it every day, it's a conversation you have with the Master. Always refer to Him as your Heavenly Father, or Jesus, or with another honorable name. You have a personal relationship with Him, but keep in mind He is your Savior, and you need to show respect for His holiness. If you are a parent, you want your children to call you by a respectful name. He wants to be recognized for who He is. The Lord is kind, gentle, and loving, but He demands your respect. When you have

71

this perspective, you will want to seek Him in prayer often and on a regular basis. Don't let days go by without kneeling in prayer. You need to speak to Him every day. It doesn't matter if it's in the morning, in a prayer closet, or on the way to work. Check in often. "Let us therefore come boldly unto the throne of grace, that we may obtain mercy, and find grace to help in the time of need" (Hebrews 4:16 KJV).

➤ Thank Him and Ask for Forgiveness: A grateful heart is the best place to start. Start your prayers by giving Him glory for the many blessings He has given you and for previous answered prayers. Thank Him for all the blessings and for the prayers He specifically did not answer for your own protection or because He had a better plan in mind. Sometimes you want certain things and are denied. Thank Him for salvation and for what He is about to do for you. Always make sure everything is clear between you and God. If you have done something that you know you should not have done, ask for His forgiveness as soon as possible, and ask Him to show you if you are doing anything to hinder His grace.

➤ Listen More than You Talk: Your prayer life is not a wish list, and God is not a genie in a bottle. But He does want to hear your needs, and He knows what is best for you. Ask for His direction and how to proceed when life becomes uncertain. Then wait. This might be difficult and even awkward, but it's important. Don't get ahead of His plan; rather, patiently wait on His timing. Don't just whip off your demands and say amen. Ask in faith, trust His Word and promises, and remember to listen to the sweet whisper of the Holy Spirit.

➤ Eliminate Distractions: Distractions are the most effective trick in the devil's playbook. You might try to pray while the television is blaring in the next room. Or you might be on your knees when your phone buzzes. Do your best to find a quiet time and place for your conversations with the Lord. Look for the best opportunities to be alone. If you take your spouse out to a romantic dinner, you want the focus to be on the two of you. The same goes for Christ. Allow for an intimate relationship so you can talk with Him in peace.

➤ Memorize Scripture: You enhance your prayer life when you quote phrases from the Bible as you speak to the Father. You will also understand your prayer life better when you reinforce your prayers with God's Word. Take just a few moments each day to try to learn your favorite Scripture verses. This will also give you more authority when you seek His face, and it will help when you order the devil to flee from your presence.

When LSU scored the game-winner against Auburn, the stadium shook, and the reaction was equivalent to an actual earthquake. When you seek the Lord in prayer every day, your life can explode with the power of the Holy Spirit. Make it a daily habit to focus on your quiet time with God in order to get as much spiritual power, strength, and wisdom as possible.

DAY 15
WHAT'S YOUR LEGACY?

November 16, 2013: Auburn 43, Georgia 38

One generation shall commend your works to another,
and shall declare your mighty acts. —Psalm 145:4

The miracle in Jordan-Hare is an example of what can happen when you make the effort and execute the plan.

Auburn was down 38–37 to their oldest rival Georgia.

Thirty-six seconds was all that was left in regulation, and Auburn was pinned back on its own twenty-seven-yard line.

To make matters worse, it was fourth down and eighteen yards to go to move the chains.

The situation was bleak, and defeat loomed over Jordan-Hare Stadium.

Coach Gus Malzahn called a play named "Little Rock," something he drew up some years earlier when he was coaching high school football. It was designed to send a receiver long on a post route to draw defenders away, while a second receiver goes far enough to get the first down.

The intended target was sophomore Sammie Coates while Ricardo Louis was the decoy.

Louis dreamed of making the big play and was fueled by wide receiver coach Dameyune Craig's challenge all year to leave a legacy.

Quarterback Nick Marshall took the snap and dropped back in the pocket.

Coates was wide open as expected, but Marshall's instincts took over, and he stepped up and heaved the ball downfield toward Louis, who was in triple coverage.

Fans held their breath as the ball traveled about fifty yards in the air. At first, it appeared to be thrown too far for Louis to grab.

But Georgia safety Tray Matthews jumped to try to make a game-saving interception.

Fellow Bulldog defender Josh Harvey-Clemons also went for the pass, but he tipped the pigskin and caused it to ricochet off Matthews's helmet.

That changed the direction of the ball and allowed Louis time to catch up with the overthrown pass.

At first, he could not handle the ball, but he was able to locate it over his shoulder.

He tried to bring the ball under control and bobbled it at the fifteen-yard line, but he gained full possession inside the ten-yard line and scampered into the end zone for the touchdown.

The miraculous seventy-three-yard game-winning score made the crowd go crazy with excitement.

With that play, Louis cemented his legacy in Auburn football history. He ran the route and did not give up on the play, even when defenders surrounded him.

How will people remember you? What one act are you known for?

What you have learned and received and heard and seen in me—practice these things, and the God of peace will be with you. —Philippians 4:9

WAR EAGLE

Life is funny. You can live your entire life by the rules, and no one may notice. But one act can define your legacy and leave a memory you may never be able to outlive. This can be good or bad depending on the act. Jackie Smith was an outstanding five-time Pro-Bowl receiver for the St. Louis Cardinals and Dallas Cowboys, and he is widely remembered for dropping a touchdown pass in Super Bowl XIII that might have helped Dallas win. Instead, Pittsburgh won the game. This is one example of how one event may define you. Ricardo Louis will always be associated with the miracle at Jordan-Hare for his heroic catch. What have you done to leave a positive legacy?

RIDE FOR THE BRAND

Are you content to work a job, raise a family, and enjoy retirement? Or do you want more out of your Christian journey and want to make a difference? You must ask yourself what impact you wish to make. Louis had a desire to work hard to make the play. He put forth the effort and was in the right spot at the right time, just how the play was designed. Here are some ways you can get the most out of your walk with Christ and leave a legacy for others to follow:

➤ Be Faithful: When I played high school sports, my mom and dad never missed a game. Every time I glanced in the stands they were there. I tried my best to do the same for my boys and was successful 95 percent of the time. This is one of the fondest memories I have of my parents—they were always there for me. I tried my best to be that example for my two sons. I am aware there are work obligations that might cause you to miss a few of your kids' events, but for the most part, make the effort to attend. They will remember your dedication. Will you be there for them?

➤ Donate Your Time: Giving back is more important than taking. There is nothing wrong with spending time on the golf course or on the lake fishing. But do you also spend time helping others? Could you give an hour each week at a soup kitchen or a homeless shelter and move some of your recreational activities to the back burner? Of course you can. You must possess the desire and drive to work for God. It's not always glamorous, but it can make a big difference.

➤ Start a Ministry: This is something that can begin at any time the Holy Spirit leads. I did not begin my writing ministry until I was fifty. I had the desire but finally sold out to God and jumped all in. I don't do it with a halfway attitude; I give it my all. Let the Lord speak to you and use your willingness and talents to serve Him.

➤ Show Compassion: Pray with a friend at the altar or buy some groceries for a neighbor in need. Never show compassion to gain recognition, but rather do it to be an ambassador for Christ. People you help may not know your name, but they will see Christ in you and know who you serve. Make time to visit patients and their families in a Hospice unit or support a charity each month with your paycheck. "Put on then, as God's chosen ones, holy and beloved, compassionate hearts, kindness, humility, meekness, and patience" (Colossians 3:12).

➢ Testify: A testimony is the most important legacy you can leave behind. When you pass away, give your family the peace and comfort of knowing they will see you again someday in eternity. Make sure others know that you love and serve God. There may be some you come into contact with who don't know all the details of your salvation, but they know there is something that sets you apart, and they want what you have. Always strive to do the right thing, treat others with love and kindness, and make others see you "do the right thing." All of this will leave a long-lasting impact on those who knew you.

You don't have to make the game-winning catch like Louis did, but if you can, go for it! Play the game by the rules, give your time and money, and live a pure and holy life. Your children will remember you for all the right things.

DAY 16
BREAK THE STREAK

October 31, 2009: Auburn 33, Ole Miss 20

But thanks be to God, who gives us the victory through
our Lord Jesus Christ. —1 Corinthians 15:57

The outlook for the rest of the 2009 season was bleak.

Auburn had lost three straight games and fallen out of the
top twenty-five rankings.

The game fell on Halloween, and fans were asked to
wear navy blue instead of orange to give the stadium a dark
atmosphere, although kickoff was set before noon.

Ole Miss came into Jordan-Hare Stadium ranked twenty-
fifth and looked to give the Tigers their fourth consecutive loss.

The Rebels set the tone early and drove down the field to
score on their first possession.

Auburn countered with a Wes Byrum field goal, then took a
halftime lead of 10–7 into the locker room after Darvin Adams
hauled in a twenty-eight-yard pass from Chris Todd.

Both teams came alive in the third quarter and scored a
combined total of thirty-six points.

Auburn dominated and whipped off twenty-one points.
Kodi Burns found Tommy Trott for a fourteen-yard scoring

strike, followed by an exciting interception return by Walter McFadden to put the lead at 24–7 with 11:25 to go in the third.

Ben Tate then rumbled fifty-three yards for the Tigers with 7:42 left on the third quarter clock to increase the lead to 31–7.

The Rebels found some life when they returned the kickoff for a touchdown, then scored again when Dexter McCluster romped seventy-nine yards on the first play of their next possession.

Auburn dug down and blocked the extra point kick, and Demond Washington ran it back ninety-eight yards for two points.

The Tigers rebounded from three losses and knocked off a top twenty-five team to put them on track to finish the year 8–5 under first-year coach Gene Chizik, who developed a strategy to win the game.

What is your plan to fight the forces of evil? Are you in a losing skid?

> Every athlete exercises self-control in all things. They do it to receive a perishable wreath, but we are imperishable. —1 Corinthians 9:25

WAR EAGLE

The devil's game plan is simple: steal, kill, and destroy. He doesn't play fair and will take cheap shots to bring you down. He wants to give you a losing season in hopes that your team will fold. You might be going through a valley of losses and have a top twenty-five team coming in to play against you. Maybe you feel hopeless and anticipate another defeat. You might be going through a personal challenge or some negative situations at work. Satan may have thrown in a few health problems and spread lies about you to your friends. These situations are real and sometimes can overwhelm you.

RIDE FOR THE BRAND

This is not your heavenly coach's first game. He has a strategy to win. But first, like all well-prepared players, you have to do your homework too. You must study game film of your opponent and read the scouting report. In other words, read your Bible every day. Watch the game film by spending time in prayer and in the house of God. The devil will fight you every step of the way and will not follow the rules. In case you don't already know, here are some of his best ways and tactics to bring you down. Don't fall for them.

➢ Division: If Satan can squeeze a wedge between you and your spouse, children, or friends, then he has a chance to win. He will use a full arsenal to win this battle by weaponizing hatred, jealousy, dissension, envy, and temptation to get his way. You must recognize the game plan and have a strategy to counteract everything he brings against you. Ask the Holy Spirit to substitute with peace, joy, love, mercy, and grace. They will help you to win the struggle.

➢ Discouragement: The devil loves to use this one. You have lost three games, and now he wants you to just give up and throw in the towel. He wants to bring you to a point where you don't want to take the field anymore and will use mistakes to try to make you feel lousy, worthless, and overwhelmed. You must look to God for comfort and realize how much He loves you.

➤ Arrogance: The devil will try to make you think you are invincible and better than other people in an effort to convince you that you don't need God anymore. It is vital for you to stay humble and lean upon God to solve your problems and give you the strength to carry on. Pride has no place in your game plan. While it is fine to be proud of your family and have self-confidence in your talents and abilities, you should always strive for humility, fear of God, and respect His mighty power in your life. Arrogance is an obstacle to serving God and helping others. "Talk no more so very proudly, let not arrogance come from your mouth; for the LORD is a God of knowledge, and by him actions are weighed" (1 Samuel 2:3).

➤ Morality: Satan makes many things enticing in an attempt to lure you into his traps. He may tempt you with money, sex, or other ways to ambush you and draw you away from God. You may believe you are ten-feet tall and bullet proof, but this is when you become the most vulnerable to the snares that Satan will have waiting for you just around the corner. When you invite temptation and put yourself in situations you know are questionable, you put yourself and your family at risk. Don't meet someone of the opposite sex for coffee alone, and don't think about

risking your savings by gambling. When the devil's enticements come your way, double down on your prayer life,
and read God's Word even more to bring you closer to
God and help you win the battle.

➤ Bitterness: When you allow discouragement to go
unchecked, you can grow bitter toward others and begin
to wallow in self-pity. The more this continues, the
stronger hold the devil will have on you, and you must
let it go and surrender to God. Pray for Him to remove
all the hurt and hostility, and let Him call the plays. Leave
it to God to deal with the person who wronged you.
Forgiveness will bring you sweet peace and rest and help
you move forward to a new chapter.

A losing streak can be hard to break because it plays with your
head at some point. Doubts creep in and make you ask, "Will
I ever win again?" Auburn was on the cusp of a fourth straight
loss but recognized the opponent's strategy and put together
a game plan to win the contest. Your game plan should be to
stay in the Word of God, attend church, pray, and serve others.
These are the ingredients for victory in Christ.

DAY 17
BE THE DIFFERENCE

October 12, 1985: Auburn 59, Florida State 27

And let us not grow weary while doing good, for in due season we shall reap if we do not lose heart. — Galatians 6:9 NKJV

Florida State strolled into Jordan-Hare Stadium ranked number four in the nation. A win against a former number-one team Auburn, who had fallen to twelfth, would be favorable in the polls.

But Seminoles Coach Bobby Bowden found out right away that the Tigers came to win.

Auburn's senior sensation Bo Jackson racked up 176 yards rushing on thirty carries to lead his team to a 59–27 drudging of Florida State.

"Bo Jackson was the difference in the game," Bowden told the media. "He's one of the greats of all time."

Jackson wasted little time and darted fifty-three yards just two minutes into the game to put Auburn ahead 7–0.

Later in the game, he rambled thirty-five yards to boost the lead to 31–17.

Florida State backup quarterback Eric Thomas tried to put the Seminoles back in the game when he set up a score with a forty-eight-yard pass to Hassan Jones, which narrowed the lead to 31–24 in the third quarter.

But Auburn roared back by whipping off four touchdowns to put the game out of reach.

Jackson lived up to his reputation as the nation's leading rusher as he led the Tigers to the lopsided win. He was the difference in the game, and Florida State could not contain the running back. You may think the circumstances of your situation point to certain failure. But you can make a difference and lead your team to victory.

Trust in the LORD, and do good; dwell in the land, and feed on His faithfulness. —Psalm 37:3 NKJV

WAR EAGLE
Are you content to just get by in your Christian journey? Are you satisfied to go through the motions and be the one who just goes to church and sits on the sidelines? If so, you may be missing out on God's blessings in your life. Jesus has something great in store for you to do, but you must be sold out and willing to obey His directions.

RIDE FOR THE BRAND
Do you have a deep desire to go to the next level with the Lord? Maybe you want to have a positive impact on others, but you can't settle on what the Master has in store for you and your life. You have spent hours in prayer and in conversations with your pastor. Be patient, and let Him speak to you and open the

right doors. Maybe you have it on your heart to take a mission trip or be an assistant Sunday school teacher. No matter what, let the Lord lead you. Here are some possible ways you can make a difference for Christ:

➤ Volunteer: When you give God your time, one of the most valuable assets you possess, God takes note and honors your sacrifice. You can volunteer at a food bank, homeless shelter, or at church-related events. You can volunteer to pick up trash after a Friday night high school football game or ring bells for the Salvation Army at Christmas. The possibilities are unlimited. "For God is not unjust to forget your work and labor of love which you have shown toward His name, in that you have ministered to the saints, and do minister" (Hebrews 6:10 NKJV).

➤ Minister: Find what you are passionate about, and ask God to open doors for you to use your talents for Him. Your ministry doesn't have to dictate a large following but can be small and impactful. You could begin a card ministry and send out encouraging notes to those who need a boost. Your ministry might involve visiting patients in a local nursing home. You might even start a monthly Bible study or post inspirational blogs on social media. Perhaps your ministry it to set a positive example in front of everyone you meet and greet them with a smile. Your ministry is yours, and the sole purpose is to let others see Christ in you.

➤ Mentor: There are many young people who do not have strong role models in their lives. You can step in and fill this role for someone to be there to offer direction and guidance in this crazy world. Don't let this experience take away from your parenting responsibilities, but rather strive to be the example for others to see, and take some young people under your wings to show them Christ in your life.

➤ Lead: This begins at home and spreads to opportunities to prove your leadership in your church and community. But first, set the positive example with your own family. Treat your spouse with respect, and teach your children right from wrong. You are not instructed to be their best friend, but you must be a parent who enforces rules for their own good. Set boundaries, and show your children love just as your Heavenly Father loves you. When you establish limits and show you mean business for their own good, they will respect it even though they might balk at first. A leader does not dictate but encourages and demonstrates unconditional love. "Be diligent to present yourself approved to God, a worker who does not need to be ashamed, rightly dividing the word of truth" (2 Timothy 2:15 NKJV).

Set your mind and heart to make a difference for your spouse and children as well as to your church family and community. Bo Jackson was a force on the field, and Florida State had no answer. You can also be the example for others to follow. Make up your mind to do good for God.

DAY 18
DON'T BE SNEAKY

November 11, 2000: Auburn 29, Georgia 26

So that we would not be outwitted by Satan; for we are
not ignorant of his designs. —2 Corinthians 2:11

A spot in the Southeastern Conference title game was at stake for
this mid-November matchup of the oldest rivalry in the South.

Jordan-Hare Stadium was packed to watch number
twenty-two Auburn face off against number fourteen Georgia.

The Bulldogs jumped out early and claimed a 13–3 lead
at the end of the first half, after Damon Duval's kick put the
Tigers on the board.

But Auburn answered after the intermission and whipped off
twenty straight points to take a 23–13 lead in the final quarter.

Georgia responded and scored ten points in the final
minutes and tied the game when Billy Bennett connected on a
nineteen-yard field goal with forty seconds left.

The contest went into overtime, where the Bulldogs scored
a field goal to take the 26–23 lead.

Auburn's Rudi Johnson, who rushed for a total of 152
yards, gained twenty-one in overtime, and put his team in
scoring position at the one-yard line.

The stage was set, and quarterback Ben Leard followed his
hefty line and crossed the goal line to score the game-winning
touchdown off a quarterback sneak.

Auburn defeated Alabama the following week to secure its spot in the SEC Championship game.

The Bulldogs fell victim to a quarterback sneak. This play is difficult to defend because the signal caller often catches the defense off guard and snaps the ball from a quick count. He then stays low and uses his blockers up front to gain the one or two yards needed to gain.

Unless the defense is aware, a quarterback sneak is successful in its goal.

The devil is also sneaky and will use whatever it takes to get what he wants.

Does your defense protect you against Satan's evil tactics?

Submit yourselves therefore to God. Resist the devil, and he will flee from you. —James 4:7

WAR EAGLE

As a believer, you are always a target for Satan. His entire game plan is to destroy you and your family. He doesn't want to just win in overtime, but he has a deep, dark desire to crush you by seventy-five points. If he can accomplish this, he will knock you out of contention for your conference title game. The devil does not play fair and will use every tool at his disposal to pick off your pass attempts and make you fumble.

RIDE FOR THE BRAND

Christians are not exempt from facing spiritual battles, but some attacks may be more dramatic than others. The devil will place a small obstacle in front of you before he rushes you with a backside blitz. You might not even realize it most of the time, but these forces are real. They will lull you to sleep with complacency and take advantage of you when you least expect it to happen. A good coach will scout the opponent weeks before each game and have a plan in place for most situations. You too must be familiar with your opposition. How can you effectively fight the enemy if you don't understand how dirty he plays? Just like a coach prepares his team for battle, you too must be aware how and when the rival will strike. In today's fast-paced society, it might be easy to lose focus and not recognize the game plan of the enemy. The world is full of distractions to keep your mind off spiritual matters. How can you prepare for Satan's next attack? Educate yourself on the devil's modus operandi, and follow this scouting report:

➤ He Is a Liar: The devil will tell you anything you wish to hear. He spends a lot of time whispering lies into your ear. He will tell you that God doesn't love you, you don't matter, you don't have a chance to survive, no one cares for you, you are ugly, and you have no worth in life. He is a liar! Remember that you are a child of the King, and nothing he tells you can change that. "Put on the whole armor of God, that you may be able to withstand against the schemes of the devil" (Ephesians 6:11).

➤ He Is a Master Disguiser: He will come to you in many fashions to entice you to sin. He might mask himself as a glamorous job that will take you away from friends and loved one. He could appear to you in the form of a glass of alcohol and tell you it's okay to consume just once. No matter how attractive his offers might be, you should always consult the Lord before a decision. What might appear to be a small choice could impact your life in the worst way. "In their case the god of this world had blinded the minds of the unbelievers, to keep them from seeing the light of the gospel of the glory of Christ, who is the image of God" (2 Corinthians 4:4).

➤ He Will Tempt You: Even if you are ranked in the top twenty, you are no match for the ways of the devil. You might be on a business trip, and he could introduce you to someone who could destroy your home. He might use money to lure you away from your morals. The grass is never greener on the other side. Be aware, stay strong in the Word of God, and consult with godly friends on a regular basis to help you remain accountable. "And no wonder, for even Satan disguises himself as an angel of light" (2 Corinthians 11:14).

➤ He Will Steal from You: He wants to take away the joy, happiness, and peace you have in Christ. But this will not be a quick theft. He will take his time and slowly take away from you a little at a time. He will use emotions like bitterness and hate to rob you of your joy. But most of all, he wants to take your soul. He is a thief.

➤ He Will Lead You Down a Path of Destruction: He will try to smack you in the face with failure before you know what has even happened. When you allow him to gain control of a small portion of your life, it won't be long until he has it all. Sin will always take you further than you had planned. You cannot give him one yard because he will advance and gain the first down.

Your responsibility is to know your opponent's tactics inside and out. You can do this by going to church on a regular basis, reading your Bible every day, and praying daily. Don't allow Satan to catch your defense off guard. Be alert, watch carefully for his sneaky attempts to deceive you, and trust in God to help you head him off at the pass.

DAY 19
RECOVER THE FUMBLE

November 12, 2005: Auburn 31, Georgia 30

Repent therefore, and turn back, that your sins may be blotted out. —Acts 3:19

Auburn needed a big play.

The Tigers trailed by two late in the final quarter. They had the ball on their own thirty-five-yard line with 3:25 left in regulation on the game clock.

Fourth down and ten to go.

Quarterback Brandon Cox dropped back and fired a pass to Devin Aromashodu in the middle of the field. The receiver pulled in the football and dashed sixty-two yards toward the goal line.

But he lost the ball when it was knocked loose at the Bulldog three-yard line and bounced into the end zone.

Courtney Taylor pounded on the ball for Auburn, which allowed them to retain possession where the ball came out.

Georgia's defense held three downs and forced an Auburn field goal attempt.

John Vaughn nailed the attempt with six seconds left on the clock to give number fifteen-ranked Auburn the 31–30 upset win over number nine-ranked Georgia.

The game was a fast-paced contest that featured high-powered offensive performances.

The Tigers tallied 506 yards of offense while Georgia whipped off 446 yards. Cox was efficient in the air with 279 yards passing while Georgia's quarterback was impressive with 306 yards in the air.

Auburn's running back, Kenny Irons, put the Tigers on the board in the first quarter. He romped thirty yards up the middle to cap off a ninety-two-yard drive that took thirteen plays.

From there, both teams went back and forth in a track-meet style game that featured several lead changes.

Irons finished the game with 179-yards rushing on thirty-seven carries to increase to five straight games with more than one hundred yards rushing.

Aromashodu's performance of 135 yards receiving on four catches was important, but his miscue could have cost the team the game. The wide receiver from Miami, Florida, did not intend to lose control of the pigskin, but it happened.

Taylor's heads-up fumble recovery made it possible for Auburn to win. It erased what could have been a disaster of the play.

Have you had to make a recovery to win the game?

Did you ever lose control of the ball after making a big play? Who bailed you out?

Then he adds, "I will remember their sins and their lawless deeds no more." —Hebrews 10:17

WAR EAGLE

You might be cruising along in life and racing toward the end zone with the win in sight. Out of nowhere, a safety catches you and hits you hard enough to jar the ball loose. You can only watch as the pigskin bobbles into the end zone. Who will recover it for you? Who hit you? What does the future hold? Perhaps you were placed in a tense situation at work and your temper got the best of you and made you fumble. Maybe you are out of town on business all alone and in a situation where no one will know if you go against your convictions. You might be in a circumstance where your reputation can be damaged. Will you fumble?

RIDE FOR THE BRAND

Wrong decisions are made every day. How you learn from your mistakes and handle the backlash will determine your integrity. Players, no matter how good and talented they are, will make errors in judgment on the field. But reactions to your blunders will determine if your team can come back to win or not. Teammates are also there to help one another through difficult challenges. Here are some ways you can overcome your fumbles from the past. They might seem obvious, but they are important steps:

> Forgive Yourself: This step is perhaps the hardest. People know that God will forgive them of their sins, but many have trouble forgiving themselves. Some people put higher standards on themselves than the Lord even does. Always remember that the Savior forgives and forgets. The devil will issue constant reminders of your past along the way to try to rob you of your joy, but trust in God to deliver you from all guilt and shame and give you peace. "If we confess our sins, he is faithful and just to forgive us our sins and to cleanse us from all unrighteousness" (1 John 1:9).

➤ Don't Look Back: When a running back is going for the end zone and glances back, he is caught or vulnerable to the defense. Once the play is over and blown dead by the referee, the clock begins to tick for the next play. Looking back does no good for anyone. When it's over, move on and call the huddle for the next series.

➤ Acknowledge: After you have forgiven yourself for a misstep, own up to it and don't pass the blame to someone else. If you need to seek forgiveness from another person, then apologize and make restitution if needed. If the other party involved chooses not to forgive, then it's off your shoulders. Do what is right and expected from God. "And whenever you stand praying, forgive, if you have anything against anyone, so that your Father also who is in heaven may forgive you your trespasses" (Mark 11:25).

➤ Learn: Messing up teaches us valuable lessons for the future. You will gain valuable knowledge and experience from your mistakes. Make a commitment to remember these experiences so you don't let history repeat itself.

➤ Start Fresh: Run up to the line of scrimmage, and call the signal to snap the ball. The most important play is the next one. Get busy and gain back the ground you lost. Something good can come from a slipup. In this case, Courtney Taylor was able to recover the ball and retain possession for Auburn. For a split second, Tiger fans might have gasped for air and anticipated a Bulldog win. But it all worked out in the end.

Mistakes will happen in life at the worst times. Make sure your focus is on the Lord, and be ready to kick the game-winning field goal after He recovers your fumble.

DAY 20
MAKE A STATEMENT

October 16, 2004: Auburn 38, Arkansas 20

Now I plead with you, brethren, by the name of our
Lord Jesus Christ, that you all speak the same thing,
and that there be no divisions among you, but that you
be perfectly joined together in the same mind and in
the same judgment. —1 Corinthians 1:10 NKJV

The Auburn Tigers sent a message early in the first quarter.

With 13:50 left in the opening stanza, quarterback Jason
Campbell connected with wide receiver Devin Aromashodu in
the middle of the field.

The speedy receiver outran the defenders for a sixty-seven-
yard touchdown, set up as a flea-flicker play.

Campbell pitched the ball to Cadillac Williams, who tossed
it to Courtney Taylor, who then flipped it back to Campbell,
who fired it to Aromashodu.

The play drew in the defense, which fell for the fakes and
allowed Aromashodu to be open.

Auburn scored on its next four possessions and had a 30–0
lead with just over four minutes to play in the first half.

Taylor hauled in a thirty-yard touchdown pass from
Campbell, which was followed by a one-yard plunge by Ronnie
Brown for the 24–0 lead.

Williams went in from two-yards out to cap a seventy-three-yard, eight-play drive for the 30–0 advantage.

Arkansas did not know what hit them and struggled the entire game; however, they did manage to score twenty points.

The Tigers caught them off guard in the opening drive and poured it on over the entire game. They set the tone early and sent a message that Auburn was serious about winning the Southeastern Conference matchup.

Campbell had a career-best with 297 yards and three touchdowns, while the running game pounded out more than 170 yards on the ground.

What message do you send with your Christian witness? Do people know about the God you serve?

Do you set the tone early and do things that let others know about your salvation?

> Therefore I exhort first of all that supplications, prayers, intercessions, and giving of thanks be made for all men, for kings and all who are in authority, that we may lead a quiet and peaceable life in all godliness and reverence. —1 Timothy 2: 1–2 NKJV

WAR EAGLE

When you meet someone for the first time, does it take you long to let them know you are a Christian? Perhaps you have a new neighbor next door or a coworker was reassigned to the office next to you. Making a first impression is important and can help you establish yourself as a true witness for Christ.

Day 20: Make a Statement

RIDE FOR THE BRAND

It may be awkward for you to engage with a person you don't know well about your spiritual beliefs right off the bat. But then again, what better time to let them know how you feel about certain topics? You can express yourself and espouse your convictions in a polite and respectful way. The last thing you want to do is alienate a person you just met. However, when sensitive subjects come up, be sure to stay true to your convictions. Here are some ways you can let your light shine without coming across as overbearing.

➤ Keep a Proper Perspective: When you look at the big picture, you are encouraged to love one another. This does not mean you let people walk all over you or say rude things to you. It means to be considerate and polite to others when you can. Leave a tip for your server at a restaurant or make sure the person who delivers your mail every day receives a Christmas gift from you. Little things can make a big difference when you keep the right attitude.

➤ Listen More and Speak Less: This is sound advice for anyone but especially for a person of faith. When you are involved in a conversation at work that might revolve around church and Christians, be sure to hear the other person's opinion before you begin to talk back. Listen. They might have something important to say. Don't interrupt, but when you do speak, use kind words that explain your position with love and conviction. "Know this, my beloved brothers: let every person be quick to hear, slow to speak, slow to anger" (James 1:19).

> Keep Your Tongue Contained: Don't lose your temper and say something you might regret. Or don't spout off when you don't understand the entire situation. Once bad words are spoken, they cannot be put back in your mouth. Use wise judgment, and make sure your temper is turned over to the Lord.

> Treat Everyone with Respect: If you want others to respect you, then you must be the one to demonstrate respect up front. If someone puts you down or makes fun of you for your beliefs, then you might have to walk away and seek God's guidance.

> Put Others First and Yourself Last: This is the best way to let everyone know you are a Christian. If you grab the last bar of soap at a store and a person comes up and wanted the same one, let them have it. Let someone get ahead of you if you are stuck in traffic. Be polite and considerate when you are around others. If a coworker takes your parking spot, then find another one. Let little things slide off your back, and don't fuss over insignificant circumstances. "Do nothing from selfish ambition or conceit, but in humility count others more significant than yourselves" (Philippians 2:3).

Auburn got the attention of Arkansas in the opening moments of the game. The Razorbacks could not respond and were defeated. You have to take the same approach and take a stand on biblical, social, and personal issues. Do not waiver, and do not bend.

DAY 21

HANG ON

September 28, 2002: Auburn 37, Syracuse 34

But test everything; hold fast what is good.
—1 Thessalonians 5:21

The game was not supposed to be close.

Syracuse rolled into Jordan-Hare Stadium as a two-touchdown underdog to favored Auburn.

But the Orangemen, who entered the game 1–2, did not listen to the prognosticators, and they showed up to play football. They booted a field goal, returned a punt eighty-five yards for a touchdown, and galloped sixty-eight-yards for a score to take an early lead.

Auburn fans were stunned because the Tigers, who were 3–1, were supposed to run all over Syracuse.

Backup quarterback Jason Campbell knew the situation looked grim and took charge. He put together scoring drives that led to twenty-four straight points and a 24–17 lead halfway through the third period.

Auburn grabbed its first lead of the game when fullback Brandon Johnson hauled in a pass from Campbell and ran thirty-four yards for the score.

Syracuse scored a touchdown to force the first of three overtimes.

Cadillac Williams turned in a brilliant performance for Auburn and posted a career-high 202 yards on the ground. He scored a touchdown in the second overtime and crossed the goal line on an eighty-yard run in the third overtime to secure the 37–34 win.

Wide receiver Marcel Willis had three catches for 113 yards for Auburn.

The Tigers were expected to win big. But the Orangemen surprised them by putting up a tough fight through three overtimes before Auburn was able to pull off the victory. Was Syracuse better prepared, or had their opponents taken them for granted? Either way, Auburn hung on to post the win. But they realized early in the contest they were in for a real test.

Sometimes people you come into contact with can put you through a trial and catch you off guard. How do you handle these surprise situations?

> For I, the LORD your God, hold your right hand; it is
> I who say to you, "Fear not, I am the one who helps
> you." —Isaiah 41:13

WAR EAGLE

Has someone in your life caught you off guard? Maybe someone close to you said words that hurt or disappointed you. Perhaps at some point your own church leaders or even your pastor has offended you. Maybe someone who served as a role model to you surprised you and let you down. All of this could lead to an avalanche of emotions and bury you with discouragement. You might even entertain thoughts of giving up on your relationship with Christ.

RIDE FOR THE BRAND

Life is packed with disappointment and events that will shock and surprise you. Be careful not to rush to judgment; we have all made mistakes. Below are some things to consider and keep in mind when your friends have let you down:

➤ Realize All Have Sinned: If someone you admire lets you down, remember that everyone is subject to sin. No one is perfect. You don't have to approve of what has taken place, but don't lift yourself up higher than them. Remember, you are also human and will make your share of mistakes. None of us are invincible or immune to failure. "For all have sinned and fall short of the glory of God" (Romans 3:23).

➤ Turn a Negative into a Positive: When a grievance is brought to light, seek God's forgiveness and ask Him to help you start over. Granted, it might take some time to heal. You can be disappointed for a short time, but this must give way to a new beginning. God can take something bad and turn it into something good. "Take no part in the unfruitful works of the darkness, but instead expose them. For it is shameful even to speak of the things that they do in secret. But when anything is exposed by the light, it becomes visible, for anything that becomes visible is light. Therefore it says, 'Awake, O sleeper, and arise from the dead, and Christ will shine on you'" (Ephesians 5:11–14).

➤ The Cross Can Bear Your Burden: When you are disappointed, don't try to handle the issue yourself. Instead, take it to God and leave it at the foot of the Cross. Christ can carry your load, no matter how big or small. No problem is too big for the Lord to solve. Leave your disappointments at the Cross, because if you store them up inside, you will invite bitterness to live with you.

➢ Be Honest: If someone has done something to hurt or disappoint you, tell them about it in love. Never do it in haste or without asking God for guidance. Think twice about posting your feelings on social media because that will have lasting ramifications. Have a genuine and honest discussion with the person, or if you are unable to meet, then consult with someone you trust to keep it between yourselves. Pray to God to help you forgive and find a reliable and trustworthy Christian friend who you can talk to for help and healing.

➢ Forgive: Everyone, including you, makes mistakes and commits sin. It's human nature. But forgiveness is essential if you want to experience peace and joy in your life. Ask God to help you through the heartbreak and to remove all bitterness.

Auburn expected an easy contest, but Syracuse startled them by putting up a fight. The Tigers had to step up their game and hold tight for the victory. You can do the same. Things might look bleak at times, and people may disappoint you in life. But don't let their actions define your own personal relationship with Christ. You can still do this. The key is to run the race and have the courage to go into overtime to be victorious. Stick with the game plan and follow God's strategy.

DAY 22
AVOID THE BITE

November 24, 2007: Auburn 17, Alabama 10

God is our refuge and strength, a very present help in trouble. —Psalm 46:1

The Iron Bowl was not on the national scene in 2007, but the game was still important for bragging rights in Alabama.

Auburn was ranked twenty-fifth and had a record of 7–4, while the Tide rolled into Jordan-Hare Stadium 6–5 and unranked in Coach Nick Saban's debut season.

Defense was the name of the game on this day, but Auburn managed to put up ten points in the first quarter, thanks in part to a Ben Tate three-yard run and a Wes Byrum field goal.

Alabama posted a touchdown and trimmed the lead to 10–7 at the half.

Auburn quarterback Brandon Cox crossed the goal line on a one-yard sneak in the final quarter to boost the lead to 17–7. Alabama could only muster a field goal.

But the play everyone remembers was not a score or a sack. Instead it involved a police dog.

Tigers defensive back Jerraud Powers broke up an Alabama pass in the end zone in the fourth quarter. He was near the back of the end zone and gave a signal similar to the one a referee makes for an incomplete pass.

Powers waived his arms, and a nearby police dog apparently interpreted it as an aggressive act.

The K-9 lunged at Powers and sunk his teeth into his left hand. Some jokingly suggested the dog was an Alabama fan.

Powers had blood coming out from under his glove and went to the locker room for treatment. In seconds, he went from celebrating a solid defensive play to being bitten by a dog.

That's how fast life can change. Has the devil ever bitten you after you have made a remarkable play in life?

> The LORD is on my side; I will not fear. What can man do to me? —Psalm 118:6

WAR EAGLE

Life definitely has its ups and downs. One day you may be celebrating good news and enjoying time with your family, and the next thing you know, you are hit with a tragedy, illness, or job loss that you did not see coming. It could even be something as insignificant as a flat tire, but it is something that distracts you from your happiness. Satan looks for every possible way to attack you where you are most vulnerable, and he does not want you to be content or to shine the light of Christ to those around you.

RIDE FOR THE BRAND

The devil will not play fair and will seek any opportunity to sink his teeth into you when you least expect him to. When life is going well, you seldom anticipate a dog bite. But this is when it often happens. Good times do not always invite misery, but the forces of evil don't like joy and happiness and will do whatever they can to prevent it. You must have your defenses up and be on guard at all times. Celebrations are in order, but be aware the devil is waiting close by, ready to take a chunk out of you. Here are some areas he's just waiting to attack:

➢ Your Spiritual Life: The devil wants to keep you away from church and Bible study. He will throw events and activities into your life to distract you and change your plans. He will also try to discourage you by tossing in lies and temptations. His plan is to take you out of your routine of going to the house of God and disrupt your daily devotions. Be committed to attend church on a regular basis. Make sure your prayer life is more important than checking your emails and text messages. "For we do not wrestle against flesh and blood, but against the rulers, against the authorities, against the cosmic powers over this present darkness, against the spiritual forces of evil in the heavenly place" (Ephesians 6:12).

➢ Your Family Life: This is Satan's main target. He wants to tear down the institution God made a priority. He will try to derail any relationship you have in your life that is meaningful. A sacred marriage and family represent the solid establishment and strength of the church. He has worked hard to spread divorce, homosexuality, and pornography throughout our nation and has used the media to get out his destructive message. He wants the relationship you have with your family to crumble.

➢ Your Personal Life: The devil will tempt you in ways you never imagined. He is sneaky and takes time to pinpoint your vulnerabilities. He will lead you down a path of destruction that is paved with enticements. They might start out small, like an invitation to play golf with your buddies on a Sunday morning when you're supposed to be at church with your family, or he might pull out the big guns and introduce a seductive coworker into your life who invites you for coffee. Stand your ground and stay with your game plan. Moments of weakness will lead to destruction. Don't go off and jump on the Internet when you are alone and expose yourself to pages you should not be viewing. And don't return inappropriate text message that can lure you into sticky situations. "And lead us not into temptation, but deliver us from evil" (Matthew 6:13).

➢ Your Work Life: Satan will use this in combination with point number two. He will throw in last-minute meetings to keep you from fulfilling your obligations to your family. It's fine to work late on occasion to meet a deadline, but when it happens often, this could develop into a problem. He will use the love of money and the things of this world to distract you from your focus. There is nothing wrong with being successful and taking your family on the vacation of a lifetime, but when this becomes your main focus, you must take note. Don't compromise your convictions to close the big deal. Maintain honesty and integrity in the workplace.

Day 22: Avoid the Bite

➤ Your Ministry Life: Every Christian has his or her own unique way to minister to others. You may not be a world-famous minister or singer, but you have a role as an ambassador for the Lord. Your ministry may not get as much notice as others, but all outreach is vital to spread the good news. The devil may try to inflict pain and suffering on you through lies and discouragement. He might try to burn you out and whisper in your ear that what you do for God does not matter. If your calling is to visit people in the hospital or send out positive cards or text messages to encourage others, remember that every way to spread God's word is important. Stay determined and focused on the work for the kingdom, "For he who is in you is greater than he who is in the world" (1 John 4:4).

Jerraud Powers did not expect a dog to reach out and bite him as he celebrated a good play. But this is the way the devil operates. He wants to bring you down from your high and take you off the field to the locker room. He does not want to see you return to the gridiron. But when you are focused on God's plan, you will be able to shake off the attacks and help your team win the Iron Bowl.

DAY 23
PICK OFF THE PASS

October 1, 1983: Auburn 27, Florida State 24

Neither give place to the devil. —Ephesians 4:27 KJV

Jordan-Hare Stadium was the host field to rival Florida State, who entered the game ranked seventeenth with a desire to upset tenth-ranked Auburn.

Kicker Al Del Greco was on target as two of his field goals helped to boost Auburn to a 20–10 lead at the half.

The Seminoles scored two touchdowns and grabbed a 24–20 lead in the final quarter.

Then Auburn quarterback Randy Campbell orchestrated a seventy-five-yard drive that culminated in a Lionel James fifteen-yard touchdown with 1:59 to play the game to give the Tigers a 27–24 lead.

Florida State tried to counter and threatened to make a go-ahead score, but linebacker Gregg Carr rose to the occasion and picked off a pass to secure the win.

Campbell threw for three touchdowns in the game and connected on twelve of twenty pass attempts. Running back Bo Jackson rumbled for 123 yards in the win, but the defense played tough and forced three Seminole turnovers.

The interception toward the end of the game stopped a drive that had momentum and served as the difference in the game.

You too can make the big play and break the devil's attempts to thwart your life.

> And we know that we are of God, and the whole world lieth in wickedness. —1 John 5:19 KJV

WAR EAGLE

If you are not careful, the forces of evil will march down the field and force the ball into your end zone. They will leave you defeated and squash your chances to win a national championship. You must be on guard at all times, and your defense should be prepared for the trick plays the devil will throw your way. The only strategy he has comes through deception. He uses lies, discouragement, and temptation to shift your defense off balance.

RIDE FOR THE BRAND

The only way to win against the devil and break his chains of sin is to make him commit a turnover. You want him to fumble, or, even better, you want to make the big interception just when he's about to score and win the game. The only way to accomplish this is to let God blitz the quarterback. This will force Satan to throw into coverage and into the hands of the linebacker, who is waiting on the pass. In order to be strong enough to win, you must first realize you are no match for the devil alone. You must allow the Master to make the big play. Repentance to God is a good move to put you in good standing with the Lord. Rather than a sign of weakness, it is a call for strength. Break through the weak areas in your life and turn them over to God. Repent and trust Christ to help you step up and pick off the pass. Here are some areas you may need God to deliver you from:

➢ Bad Language: Filthy language is a sign of what's in your heart. If the devil can put you in a situation where your first reaction is to use profanity, repent and ask God to cleanse your heart and remove these words from your vocabulary. You are an ambassador for Christ, and your speech must reflect that. Set yourself apart from the world, and shine His light with words of love. Spencer W. Kimball said, "Profanity is the effort of a feeble brain to express itself forcibly." "Let no corrupt communication proceed out of your mouth, but that which is good to the use of edifying, that it may minister grace unto the hearers" (Ephesians 4:29 KJV).

➢ Lying: The devil wants you to lie every day. He wants to put you in situations where you feel that a little white lie is okay. Honesty is difficult sometimes, but it always wins out in the end. You don't have to keep track of your lies if you tell the truth, and you won't entertain a guilty conscious if you are honest. If you have dishonesty in your life, then Satan has a first down and goal-to-go in the fourth quarter.

➢ Stealing: Theft does not always include taking an object that doesn't belong to you. You can also steal by cutting out of work early or forgetting to return something you borrowed. You rob God when you don't attend church or cut back on your devotions and prayer time. Don't steal from the Lord. "Treasurers of wickedness profit nothing: but righteousness delivereth from death" (Proverbs 10:2 KJV).

➢ Bitterness: Jealousy and bitterness can lead to a big score for the devil. He wants you to live a life of division. He wants you to be upset about the person who was awarded the promotion you thought you deserved or to harbor resentment against a person who did you wrong and lied about you. He wants you to be like him—full of bitterness. Misery loves company. When you allow hate to creep in, Satan can steal your joy and peace that only God can restore.

➢ The Appearance of Evil: Stay away from places and people that might drag you down. If you have to second guess whether or not to go to a certain venue, then don't. If you are a Christian, stay away from the bar scene. Nothing good happens in those places. If you are married, don't be seen alone with members of the opposite sex. These are common sense approaches to situations that might seem harmless on the outside, but they may lead to a questionable reputation. "Abstain from all appearances of evil" (1 Thessalonians 5:22 KJV).

You can never go wrong with asking the Lord for help. This is not a sign of weakness, but simply a recognition that you cannot handle the big loads alone. Gregg Carr stepped up and made the huge play for Auburn to secure the win. He did not sit back and wait for the receiver to make the catch and then tackle him. He stepped up and grabbed the pass. You can do the same. Recognize the threat and turn it over to the Master.

DAY 24
SOMETHING SPECIAL

December 2, 1989: Auburn 30, Alabama 20

Let me hear in the morning of your steadfast love, for in you I trust. Make me know the way I should go, for to you I lift up my soul. —Psalm 143:8

It was the first time for the Iron Bowl to be played on the Auburn University campus at Jordan-Hare Stadium. A Tiger win was in the air, and everything pointed to an Auburn (8–2) victory. It was meant to be.

The Tide (10–0) rolled into the game ranked number two in the nation and had a chance to advance and play for a National Championship.

The players on Auburn, ranked eleventh, had upset on their minds.

The opening drive for the Tigers sent a clear message: they came ready to play.

Quarterback Reggie Slack found Alexander Wright for a big gain that set up a one-yard touchdown plunge by James Joseph for the early 7–0 lead.

Alabama managed a field goal and then took a 10–7 lead on an eighteen-yard touchdown pass.

Auburn came out in the third quarter and scored when Slack connected with Shayne Wasden for a fifty-seven-yard pass play that put the ball inside the Alabama ten-yard line.

Joseph again scored on a one-yard-run for the 14–10 lead.

A field goal increased the Auburn advantage to 17–10, setting the stage for a high-scoring final period.

Darrell "Lectron" Williams scored on an eleven-yard run, and another field goal made the score 27–10.

Alabama scored a touchdown and added a field goal to cut the lead to 27–20.

The Tide tried an on-side kick, but Auburn was ready and recovered the ball with good field position.

Another Tiger field goal secured the 30–20 win, and the team celebrated a huge upset win over the Crimson Tide.

For the Auburn faithful, there was something special about this victory. Not only was it the inaugural game played at their new home stadium, but the win also knocked Alabama out of contention for the National Championship during a season that both teams shared the SEC title.

Being a follower of Christ is also special. But do you return the favor and make those around you feel important?

> Anyone who does not love does not know God, because God is love. —1 John 4:8

WAR EAGLE

When life becomes hectic and busy, it's easy to lose focus and forget to tell the important people in your life how special they are to you. You work all day and take care of issues that need to be addressed. You have activities in the evening such as helping your spouse around the house or assisting your children with their homework. Life can be a blur when there are also activities planned on the weekends. You time is precious, and you can sometimes feel as though you are being pulled from all sides. But be sure to let others know how much you appreciate them. Don't take them for granted, and make it a priority to give them roses before it is too late.

RIDE FOR THE BRAND

You might have a generous boss at work who puts in long hours along with you to get the job done sooner. Or perhaps your spouse goes above and beyond to take care of you. They need to know you appreciate them. Your kids long for your approval too. Are you there for them? Do you make them feel special? Here are some ways you can acknowledge all of them:

➢ Compliment Others: Make sure you offer a flattering remark or a congratulations to your coworkers and family members as often as possible. Consider setting a measurable goal, like complimenting three people a day. Don't make things up, but make a point to give someone their dues if they have earned them. Maybe it's been a while since you told your spouse she has a nice smile. Tell others how important they are to your life, and thank them for being there for you.

➢ Give Words of Encouragement: Saying, "Thank you," "You can do this," or, "Keep up the good work," can make a big difference to someone at the right time. You can be the reason your friend continues on his diet or goes to the gym when he doesn't feel like going. You can also be an inspiration for others to go to church. When they see you smile all the time and in a good mood, you can tell them it's because God gives you joy in your life. People are drawn to encouragement. Be the reason others want to be a Christian.

➤ Give Credit and Praise for a Job Well Done: Your spouse, children, friends, or coworkers all like to know that hard work pays off. If your children do well in school or on a project, let them know you are proud of them. If your spouse has worked hard to make sure the house or lawn looks nice, tell them. Don't be jealous when coworkers get attention for finishing a project well. Congratulate them, and use their example as an inspiration to help you be a better employee.

➤ Listen: If friends or loved ones need to talk, remember that you don't always have to know the answers. Be sure to listen to them intently, look them in the eye, and pray with them about their burdens. Don't be so focused on what you're going to say next that you don't even hear what they are saying. Sometimes it just makes people feel better to talk about the situation and express their feelings. Let them know they can trust you to remain confidential, and keep them in your prayers.

➤ Pray with and for Others: Prayer is the best thing you can do for anyone. When you take them to the Lord in prayer, you make them feel special. They may not even know you do this, but they will receive a blessing from God, and so will you. If you have a friend who has confided in you, ask them if it's okay to pray with them. If they say yes, then pray with them aloud. Speak words of life and Scripture to them, and trust God to bring them through their situation. If you make a commitment to pray for them, remember to put them on your daily prayer list. Check up on them from time to time, and remind them that you are still praying for them. "And so, from the day we heard, we have not ceased to pray for you, asking that you may be filled with the knowledge of his will in all spiritual wisdom and understanding" (Colossians 1:9).

You don't have to buy expensive gifts to let others in your life know they are special. But when you make an effort to compliment them, encourage them, praise them, listen to them, and pray with them, you will make them feel more special than the first win over Alabama at Jordan-Hare Stadium.

DAY 25
OVERCOME THE ODDS

October 16, 1993: Auburn 38, Florida 35

Yet in all these things we are more than conquerors though Him who loved us. —Romans 8:37 NKJV

No one gave Auburn a respectable chance to win the game.

The number-four ranked Florida Gators made their way up to Jordan-Hare Stadium from the Sunshine State and expected to take a bite out of Auburn, who entered the contest ranked nineteenth.

Florida, 6–0–1, featured a high-powered offense that scored in a hurry and often.

College football analysts had all but awarded the National Championship to the Gators, but the Tigers had Southeastern Conference football on their minds.

Quarterback Danny Wuerffel put Florida on the board in the first period and posted a 10–0 lead.

Another potential scoring drive was stopped when Auburn defender Calvin Jackson picked off a pass and romped ninety-five yards for the score, to cut the lead to 10–7.

The play was huge because the score could have been 17–0 in favor of Florida. Instead, the Tigers were in the game.

However, the Gators managed two more scores and took a 24–14 lead at halftime.

At the break, the Tigers made some adjustments on the offensive end and came out throwing the ball.

With thirteen minutes and forty seconds to play in the game, Auburn took its first lead and scored two touchdowns to post a 28–27 advantage.

The Tiger defense again rose to the occasion and picked off Wuerffel again, which set up a Frank Sanders nine-yard run into the end zone. Florida countered with a touchdown and made the two-point conversation to tie the game 35–35.

On Auburn's next drive, Scott Etheridge booted a forty-one-yard field goal with one minute and twenty-one seconds to play in the game and gave the Tigers a 38–35 lead.

Florida had one more chance to tie the game, but the Tiger defense stiffened and preserved one of the greatest upsets in Auburn history.

Few people gave them a chance, but they believed in themselves and got the job done.

Have you had to play the role of the underdog? Have people counted you out? Have you had to prove people wrong and show them you have what it takes to win the game?

Who is he who overcomes the world, but he who believes that Jesus is the Son of God? —1 John 5:5 NKJV

WAR EAGLE

There are no guarantees in this journey. Throughout life, you will be faced with moments that will uplift you with joy and challenge you with feelings of despair. You will experience happiness and then go through dark valleys. This can come at any time. You could have one of the most exciting days ever and come home to tragic news. Everyone will go through ups and downs. There might be times you are faced with discouragement and want to throw in the towel. Depression and anxiety can put you in the dumps.

RIDE FOR THE BRAND

When you experience difficult times, others may count you out. But your true friends and loved ones will support you and lift you up to the Lord. Don't listen to the negative comments people make or give way to rumblings from the devil. He wants you to lose and give up. As a follower of Christ, it's important not to allow obstacles in life to dampen your faith. There might be times when you will be considered an underdog to finish the race. Here are some ways you can respond and pull off the upset:

➢ Allow Love to Conquer Fear: When you run into a challenge in life, you may experience worry, anger, frustration, anxiety, and depression. These are real emotions and can take over your life if you are not careful. The key to pulling off the upset it to allow God's love to take over. Instead of focusing on the negative situation, turn to His love for you. This may not necessarily make the problem go away, but it will give you a better and more peaceful way to handle the issue. His love for you is much better and greater than any problem you might face.

➤ Keep Your Eyes on God's Power: He can do all things. You must believe this promise. He will give you strength and encouragement through the challenges you face if you ask. Jesus has the power to bring you through any trial. But you must learn to wait on His timing and be ready to give praise and glory when He shows His might. "Behold, I am the LORD, the God of all flesh. Is there anything too hard for Me?" (Jeremiah 32:27 NKJV).

➤ Trust in His Plan: Auburn stayed with the game plan and knocked off the number-two ranked Gators. Prognosticators did not give the Tigers a chance. But the team prepared and listened to their coaches to win the game. You must do the same with God. Read your Bible and pray daily. Go to church on a regular basis and seek His will. The Master's plan will be just right.

➤ Know Your Identity in Christ: Through all the good and bad times, always know God loves you, and you are His child. He will not forsake you and leave you to die. The forces of evil want you to turn away from the Lord and lose the game. But when you claim the Spirit of God in your life, you will pull off the upset. "Knowing this, that our old man was crucified with Him, that the body of sin might be done away with, that we should no longer be slaves to sin" (Romans 6:6 NKJV).

➤ Surround Yourself with Like-Minded People: Auburn did not rely on one person to win the game. Everyone on the team played a role. You must surround yourself with good teammates who will lift you up in prayer and help you along the way. Confide in close friends or your pastors, and ask them to pray with you. Allow your close friends to hold you accountable, and bear one another's burdens.

You can overcome the odds and win the big game. All you need to do is allow God's love to move into your heart and trust His power to deliver. Auburn did not let Florida's high-powered offense intimidate them. Instead, they applied the game plan and pulled off the upset. Believe in who you are as a Christian, and depend on your teammates to help you overcome the odds.

DAY 26
MAKE THE RIGHT DECISION

November 22, 1997: Auburn 18, Alabama 17

But the wisdom from above is first pure, then peace-
able, gentle, open to reason, full of mercy and good
fruits, impartial and sincere. —James 3:17

Although Alabama was having a tough season, this was still the
Iron Bowl.

Auburn was ranked thirteenth in the nation and had
a record of 8–2, while Alabama limped into Jordan-Hare
Stadium with a 4–6 mark under first-year coach Mike Dubose.

The Tide rolled to a 17–6 lead in the fourth quarter.

But Dameyune Craig orchestrated a touchdown drive and
later a field goal to cut the Alabama lead to 17–15.

Alabama had the ball and only needed a first down to run
the clock down and win the game.

Still in their own territory, Coach Dubose called a questionable screen pass.

The play—if it was run correctly—could result in a first
down. But if the pass was incomplete, then the clock stopped.

Alabama did not count on the result.

On a third-and-eight on the Alabama thirty-six yard line,
quarterback Freddie Kitchens lobbed the ball to fullback Ed
Scissum. He hauled in the pigskin, but he lost control within
seconds after Auburn's Montavius Houston hit the receiver.

Quinton Reese fell on the loose ball for the Tigers to give them new life and a chance to win the game.

Craig was able to move the ball eleven yards to the Alabama twenty-two yard line.

On third down, Auburn opted to attempt a field goal.

Jaret Holmes came in to boot the ball through the goal posts for the 18–17 win.

Auburn took advantage of a questionable call from Alabama and won the game.

The screen play did not turn out to be the best decision for the Tide.

Have you ever made a wrong decision? Who do you go to for counsel when you're not sure what to do?

Where there is no guidance, a people falls, but in an abundance of counselors, there is safety. —Proverbs 11:14

WAR EAGLE

You make choices every day. Most of them do not have tremendous consequences such as what to wear or whether or not to drink that third cup of coffee. But you have also made some important blunders. We all have. These missteps may be related to your business, personal, or spiritual life. No one intentionally makes wrong decisions, but it happens. At the end of the day, these could lead to life-changing consequences. Have you ever made an impulse buy and later regretted it? Have you ever acted out of anger and instantly wished you could take it all back? What influences the choices you make?

RIDE FOR THE BRAND

As a parent, there are some things you tell your children not to do because you know it will bring harm, such as touching a hot stove or trying to catch a bumble bee. Your past experience has prepared you to protect your family. Through the years of good and bad decisions, you have many lessons learned to pass onto the next generation. Just like we know what's best for our children, God knows what's best for us, and we should always pray for His advice. In addition, here are some other factors to consider in order to avoid a blunder:

➢ Don't Make a Decision Too Fast: Quick decisions are acceptable when the consequences are minimal. But when you are contemplating major decisions in your life, take your time to make the right choice. Depending on the circumstances, you might take minutes, hours, or even days to come to a conclusion. You must examine the consequences of your actions before making an important choice. Make it your priority to wait and seek God's advice and direction. "Wait for the LORD; be strong, and let your heart take courage; wait on the LORD" (Psalm 27:14).

➢ Don't Make a Decision in Order to Make Others Happy: People pleasing should never come into play when trying to make the right decision. Most of the time, the correct choice may not be the popular one among the crowd. Don't give in to peer pressure or try to please a friend. You need to make the decision that is best for you and your family.

➢ Don't Make a Decision Out of Anger: When you are upset, emotions can cloud your thinking and lead to overreactions, wrong decisions, and even regrets. Consider all the facts and potential consequences before you come to a final conclusion. Wait patiently on God to guide you in all areas of your life.

➤ **Don't Make a Decision Out of Fear:** When you make a decision based on fear of the unknown, you are telling God you don't trust Him, and you are almost guaranteed to fail. If the Lord has told you it will all be okay and you go against His will and act on your own, you will have to live with the outcome. Remain patient, listen to the Holy Spirit, and live by faith. If you act too soon and get ahead of God, the results might be long-lasting.

➤ **Don't Make a Decision by Yourself:** In any major life event, a decision is best reached when you consult with those who are important to you. Alabama's coaches made a decision to pass the ball when they should have kept the ball on the ground. The result was a fumble and a loss. When you are posed with a game-winning decision, do you gather input from your spouse, family, or close friends? Do you seek God's will? The other team—in this case Satan and his helpers— want you to act alone and isolate yourself from your team. Gather opinions from those who love you and want the best for you, pray to God for His will in your life, and make an educated and well-thought-out decision. "If any of you lacks wisdom, let him ask God, who gives generously to all without reproach, and it will be given him" (James 1:5).

You will face many important decisions throughout your life, and you must weigh the outcomes before you act. The wrong decision can lead to negative results. Trust the Lord to design the best play for your life, and don't throw a screen pass on third down in your own territory with the game on the line.

DAY 27
DON'T COME UP SHORT

November 16, 1996: Georgia 56, Auburn 49

But the one who endures to the end will be saved.
—Matthew 24:13

Auburn took a 28–7 lead, and victory was in sight.

Quarterback Dameyune Craig lit up the scoreboard with three touchdowns in the first half, with two going to Robert Baker, for a 28–14 lead at the break.

Georgia signal caller Mike Bobo came in off the bench halfway through the second quarter to try to rally his team.

Brian Smith had taken over the quarterback position, but Coach Jim Donnan opted to give Bobo another chance.

The move was a good one for the Bulldogs as he threw for 360 yards and two touchdowns.

The one hundredth meeting of the oldest rivalry in the Deep South became a wild shootout.

Both teams combined for 1,095 yards in the game.

Bobo connected with Corey Allen for a thirty-yard touchdown to send the game into overtime. Georgia did not have any timeouts, but officials stopped the clock to spot the ball, and Bobo was able to spike the ball and force another down. That is when he found Allen for his first career touchdown.

Auburn scored in the first overtime when Craig scrambled thirteen yards into the end zone. Georgia answered and tied the game at 35–35 to force a second overtime.

The teams traded scores over the next two extra periods, and the game was locked at 49–49.

Georgia's Torin Kirtsey plunged in from one yard out in the fourth overtime to give the Bulldogs a 56–49 lead.

The Tigers faced a fourth-down and three-yards to go for the first down inside the twenty.

Craig dropped back and had to scramble. He was tackled one yard shy of the first down marker to end the game.

His valiant effort came up short, and number-twenty Auburn fell at home.

Does this sound familiar? Have you made great strides to be an effective Christian and want to finish strong, but you have dealt with failures along the way?

> Fear not, for I am with you; be not dismayed, for I am your God; I will strengthen you, I will help you, I will uphold you with my righteous hand. —Isaiah 41:10

WAR EAGLE

A follower of Jesus Christ has one ultimate goal: eternal life in heaven. You can live your entire life serving Him and doing fantastic things for the kingdom. You may teach Sunday school or sing in the church choir. You might have an effective ministry or be content to be a silent prayer warrior. Whatever you have been called to do by the Master, you must do it with the right vision and attitude. You cannot let the attacks from the enemy force you into a fourth overtime only to come up short of your goal.

RIDE FOR THE BRAND

Throughout life, you will be faced with many challenges. You could receive devastating news from your doctor or be hit with financial issues. You might fall victim to personal relationship problems or run into unforeseen circumstances that force you to your knees. The last thing you should do is turn your back on God and come up short of your goal to reach heaven. You can finish strong and cross the goal line in life's fifth overtime. Here are some suggestions for how to keep the game alive:

➢ Stay Focused: You will be confronted with temptations and trials along your path. If you are not focused on your goals, you might be swayed to drift. The devil will throw many different formations at you to distract you along the way. But keep the goal line in view, and don't come up short.

➢ Remain Determined: Focus on your overall goal of reaching heaven, and resist the temptations that come your way. Satan wants you to glance at an attractive coworker who could eventually destroy your marriage. He wants you to linger on the Internet to look at sites you know are off limits. He wants you to return that text message that could end a relationship, and he wants you to play golf with your buddies instead of going to church. He will pull you in all different directions, but you must stay strong. Auburn athletes must work out every day to remain strong to compete. Your workout to prevent you from falling into sin's trap is to read your Bible every day, pray to the Heavenly Father for guidance, and attend church on a regular basis. Don't give in and fall short.

"Set your minds on things that are above, not on things that are on earth" (Colossians 3:2).

➤ Run for Shelter: When you are under attack and blitzed by the enemy, don't try to fight the rush alone. You can turn to the Lord in times of despair and have a core group of Christian friends who you can trust to help you through a struggle. Find comfort in the Word of God and in prayer, but also in numbers.

➤ Seek Assurance: Find a quiet space, and talk to the Lord. Ask Him to give you assurance of your salvation. Discouragement is a tool the devil uses to fight believers all the time. When this happens, look at the moment as a sign to move in closer to God. "But seek first the kingdom of God and his righteousness, and all these things will be added to you" (Matthew 6:33).

➤ Praise Him: This will give you the strength you need to make the run for the first down marker. When you lift your hands in honor of the King of kings, you fill your soul and spirit with the energy needed to gain the extra yard.

When you run to God in times of trial and temptation, you will receive guidance and the strength needed for the long journey to help you finish strong. Be prepared for overtimes in your life, and ask God for the strength to reach your goal. Don't come up short in your quest to follow Christ.

DAY 28
MAKE YOUR PRESENCE KNOWN

September 4, 2010: Auburn 52, Arkansas State 26

> But in your hearts honor Christ the Lord as holy, always being prepared to make a defense to anyone who asks you for a reason for the hope that is in you; yet do it with gentleness and respect. —1 Peter 3:15

The Auburn nation had waited for this moment.

Cam Newton made his Tiger debut against Arkansas State and left quite the impression.

The former Florida and junior college transfer quarterback took the college football world by storm when he burst onto the scene at Jordan-Hare Stadium.

He did it all and was the complete package. He was just what Auburn needed.

The six-foot-five, 235-pounder from Atlanta, Georgia, turned in a magnificent performance, and this was the sign of great things to come.

Newton connected on nine of his fourteen pass attempts for 186 yards and three touchdowns, which was impressive. But he was also a force on the ground and rushed for 171 yards and two touchdowns in fifteen carries for an average of 11.4 yards per carry.

His 357 yards of total offense demonstrated one of the best performances from a college quarterback in the Southeastern Conference. He was the real deal.

The first touchdown he threw in Auburn history was a thirty-six-yarder to Mario Fannin.

Toward the end of the first half, he galloped seventy-one yards on the ground for a score into the end zone.

Do you make your presence known as a follower of the Lord?

You see that a person is justified by works and not by faith alone. —James 2:24

WAR EAGLE

No matter if you are starting your first day on the job or near retirement, there is always time to make your presence known about the God who loves you. There is always an opportunity to proclaim your salvation and be a light to a lost and dying world.

RIDE FOR THE BRAND

If you just moved into a new neighborhood or are beginning your first day on a new job, you want to fit in and be liked. But at the same time, you want to hold to your convictions and not waiver in your relationship with God. You have a desire to be friendly and to also let everyone know you are a Christian. Here are some ways you can make your presence known:

> ➢ Be Consistent: This is the first step in making a lasting impression to others and to the Lord. Your dedication to serving Christ can help you to become a leader in your

church or community. Pay your dues, and let everyone around you know you are on this journey for the long haul. "Therefore, my beloved brothers, be steadfast, immovable, always abounding in the work of the Lord, knowing that in the Lord your labor is not in vain" (1 Corinthians 15:58).

➤ Be Active: Don't settle for life on the sidelines. Take an active role and spread the gospel. The first step to accomplish this is to pray and ask God what He wants you to do. Once He reveals His will to you, get started. Walk through the doors He opens for you. Keep in mind He doesn't have to give you a high-profile assignment, but you can share the joy of Christ with others in many ways. You can post encouraging messages on social media or visit people in the hospital and pray with them or their families. You can send out anonymous cards or gifts to people in need.

➤ Be Selfless: Give and sacrifice your time for others. Christians should lead by example and reach out with a helping hand. You can volunteer your time to charitable organizations or support them financially. You are summoned to make a difference and help those less fortunate than you. Ask God for a humble spirit and a giving heart.

➤ Be Bold: You might ask yourself how can you be bold and humble at the same time, but God can help you be both. He has not called you to be meek when it comes to proclaiming His love for humankind. You must stand in the pocket and fire the ball downfield in order to score to be an effective quarterback. The same goes for being a successful follower of Jesus. Never back down from your faith and convictions. Resist temptation, and show the world the happiness you find in serving Jesus. Never waiver in the face of the enemy. Stand for what you believe in, and let others know about the God of love whom you serve. "Proclaiming the kingdom of God and teaching about the Lord Jesus Christ with all boldness and without hindrance" (Acts 28:31).

➤ Be Ready: You can never let your guard down, because if you do, the other team will take note and call for a blitz right up the middle and sack you for a huge loss. Discouragement is one of the best tools used by the devil, and you must recognize when he pulls it out to attack you. Stay strong in prayer, and talk to God every day. Attend church on a regular basis, and read the Bible, your playbook, every day. Don't make excuses. You take time to be on social media or spend on your favorite hobby—make time for the Creator of the universe. You never know when you will be placed in a situation to witness for Him. Always be prepared to share the gospel and lead the way. "Be watchful, stand firm in the faith, act like men, be strong" (1 Corinthians 16:13).

You don't have to be flashy to get the job done. Cam Newton was a dynamic quarterback for the Tigers and used his ability and talents to lead his team. But remember that you have your own unique talents to offer to God and to others. Use them to put God's plans into action and to show everyone who you serve.

DAY 29
THE STORM WILL PASS

September 19, 2009: Auburn 41, West Virginia 30

He that dwelleth in the secret place of the most High shall abide under the shadow of the Almighty. —Psalm 91:1 KJV

The start of the game was delayed by about an hour as a storm moved through Alabama.

Fans were encouraged to seek shelter in the concourse, but many in the Tiger student section were stubborn and refused to move. They were determined to show their support.

Both the Mountaineers and the Tigers came into Jordan-Hare Stadium undefeated with records of 2–0.

When the game finally kicked off, West Virginia jumped out to a quick 14–0 lead within the first five minutes.

The Tigers regrouped and were able to counter when Wes Byrum connected on a field goal, and quarterback Chris Todd found Darvin Adams for a sixteen-yard touchdown pass.

But WVU answered and scored another touchdown to increase the lead to 21–10 at the end of the first quarter.

Auburn followed the same routine in the second quarter when Byrum kicked a three-pointer, and Todd again connected with Adams for a score to close the gap to 21–20 at the half.

Halfway through the third period and following a West Virginia score, Mario Fannin rumbled eighty-one yards for a touchdown to lead Auburn to tie the game 27–27.

The Mountaineers booted a field goal to take a 30–27 lead, but that would be the last time they scored.

Adams and Todd hooked up for a third time midway through the fourth quarter, and Craig Stevens secured the win when he intercepted a WVU pass and returned it for a touchdown.

Both teams combined to produce more than nine hundred yards of offense, but they had to wait for the thunder and lightning to pass to play the game.

Have you ever been in a personal storm and had to wait till it passed before you could score?

> He maketh the storm a calm, so that the waves thereof are still. —Psalm 107:29 KJV

WAR EAGLE

All storms are different. Some may just pour down the rain while others can be fierce with high winds, thunder, and lightning. Some cause structural damage or flooding that can lead to other issues and put lives in danger. On a personal level, you may have to battle the elements of life. These might come in the form of cancer, a job loss, more therapy for your sick child, or the loss of a relationship all caused by the devil's tornado.

RIDE FOR THE BRAND

When a storm approaches my home, I look out the window at the daunting clouds and glance at the forecast. I want to be prepared and make sure my family is safe and my possessions are secured. I want to make sure I am prepared for the worst and have a plan in place if it escalates into something major. But there are times when I have faced personal storms and was not ready for them to happen. I was caught off guard. When those moments happened, the last thing I wanted to hear was, "It's going to be okay," or, "Everything happens for a reason." Those phrases, although true, irritate me. I know what to do, and the people who told me those were trying to be supportive. It was only when I listened to their advice and turned to the One who can calm the storm that it soon passed. There was some damage, but I weathered through it and became stronger. Here are some tips to ensure your safety through the storms of life:

➢ Remind Yourself of God's Promises: The Lord will never leave or forsake you (Hebrews 13:5). You might feel overwhelmed and threatened, but dive into the Word and take comfort in knowing He will bring you through the strongest of storms.

➢ Seek Shelter: You are no match for the high winds and hard rain. You would not just stand in an open field and watch the clouds roll in. Of course, you would seek shelter for protection. In life's storms, you must do the same thing. Crawl up under God's wings, and hide in His Word, seek Him in prayer, and turn to your spiritual family for support and comfort. You are no match for the storm alone. "I will say of the LORD, He is my refuge and my fortress: my God; in him will I trust" (Psalm 91:2 KJV).

➤ Pray and Praise Your Way Though: Prayer and praise will give you peace and strength until the storm passes. Turning to God is not a sign of weakness, but it is a realization that you need Him and must depend on His grace to get you through. "Be still, and know that I am God: I will be exalted among the heathen, I will be exalted in the earth" (Psalm 46:10 KJV).

➤ Examine the Damage: You might be battered and torn from the high winds, but you are alive and able to make a comeback. The devil may have scored on you early in the game, but if you follow and trust the Lord's game plan, you can fight your way to victory. "The LORD is good, a strong hold in the day of trouble; and he knoweth them that trust in him" (Nahum 1:7 KJV).

➤ Keep Going: Auburn stayed the course and did not let a two-touchdown deficit discourage them. They kept their focus and put together drives to take advantage of sound defense to win. Had they given up early, they would have gone down in defeat. Don't be discouraged when the devil jumps out to an early lead in your storm. Keep going, and let God intercept the pass to secure your victory.

You may experience weather that threatens your faith, but know that God will take care of you if you put your trust in Him. He will help you to recover when the dark clouds finally give way to sunshine. Honor the Lord, take note of the damage the rough winds and rain caused, and use this to help you prepare for the next storm. Praise Him for taking care of you, and stay on your journey.

DAY 30
MAKE THE RIGHT CHOICE

September 29, 1990: Auburn 26, Tennessee 26

> But the wisdom from above is first pure, then peace-
> able, gentle, open to reason, full of mercy and good
> fruits, impartial and sincere. —James 3:17

Auburn, ranked third in the nation, found itself down by fifteen in the fourth quarter to fifth-ranked Tennessee.

Freshman quarterback Stan White had a monumental task in front of the eighty thousand-plus fans at Jordan-Hare Stadium.

White rallied his team and completed thirty of his fifty-six pass attempts for 338 yards and three touchdowns—all in the second half.

His efforts helped Auburn to come back and tie the game.

With one minute and fifty-six seconds to go in the final period, White connected with Greg Taylor for an eleven-yard touchdown catch.

At first, it appeared that Tennessee defender Dale Carter was going to pick off the pass, but Taylor stepped in front to make the grab.

Tigers Coach Pat Dye had a decision to make.

If he chose to go for the two-point conversion, Auburn might win—or lose if the play was not successful.

The other option was to kick the point-after and have a good chance to tie the game with a few seconds left on the clock.

A deadlock game meant each team would have a 1–0–1 Southeastern Conference record and remain in contention for the SEC Championship. A loss would mean a rough road ahead for Auburn to win the title.

The previous season, Auburn shared the SEC crown with Tennessee and Alabama.

Dye opted for the safer choice and kicked the PAT to tie the game.

But the Volunteers made a valiant effort to win and marched down the field and put themselves in field goal range with fifteen seconds left on the clock.

Tennessee's kicker missed the attempt, and the game ended in a tie.

Dye said after the game that his team played too hard to lose. A tie, instead of a loss, was a moral victory.

What do you take into consideration when you make decisions?

For I know the plans I have for you, declares the LORD, plans for welfare and not for evil, to give you a future and a hope. —Jeremiah 29:11

WAR EAGLE

An impulse buy most of the time is wrong. You let emotions and feelings guide your selections. There are times when it pays off, like when you are in line for ice cream or picking the perfect doughnut to go with your cup of coffee. But when you are faced with tougher decisions, what do you take into account? Making tough choices is never easy, no matter what stage of life you are in. You might be considering your first job offer or who to ask out on a date. Or you might be farther along in life with a job and a family, but you are considering some important changes.

RIDE FOR THE BRAND

A wrong choice can result in devastating consequences. If you get an offer for a job that pays a lot of money but will take too much time away from being with your family and going to church, then you may want to reconsider your priorities. Suppose you are having doubts about committing to a relationship because you fear the other person will hinder your spiritual growth. Do you want to live like that for the rest of your life? Most decisions you make won't have life-impacting ramifications, but some might. Here are some points to consider when you are pressed to make a choice that could impact everyone in your life:

➤ Ponder: All scenarios and options must come into play. Coach Dye looked at all possibilities and how his decision could affect his team. He chose what he felt was the best plan for his squad and their season's future. Seek out knowledge, and don't make a rash decision. Make sure you spend time in prayer, and ask God for direction and wisdom.

➤ Discuss: You should never make an important decision without advice and input from people who are important in your life. This might include your spouse, a pastor or church leader, or even your children if you are a parent. Kids will tell you the truth without prejudice. "Where there is no guidance, a people falls, but in an abundance of counselors there is safety" (Proverbs 11:14).

➢ Clarify: Sometimes when you are about to make a decision, you might battle between your mind, heart, and gut. All three might be telling you different things. Make a list of the pros and cons, study them, and ask God to help you make the right decision.

➢ Decide: Once you have prayed and asked for counsel, it's time to act. This step takes courage, but there comes a time when you have to move ahead without looking back. When you are courageous in going for what God wants you to have, He will take care of you. Have confidence that the Lord has directed your path.

➢ Accept: When the decision has been made, you will feel a sense of contentment and be ready to move ahead. Do not second guess yourself; be excited about the future. "Not that I am speaking of being in need, for I have learned in whatever situation I am to be content" (Philippians 4:11).

Coach Dye knew that if the two-point conversation failed, his team would be distraught about losing a game they had fought hard to get back into. They were down and made a valiant effort to be in a place to win. His decision was based on quick input from his coaching staff. He did not second guess and lived with the outcome. Overall, he said it was the best option for his team in that situation. Seek God's direction, and move ahead to make the right choices in your life.

DAY 31
BE A REAL CHRISTIAN

September 25, 2010: Auburn 35, South Carolina 27

For we aim at what is honorable not only in the Lord's sight but also in the sight of man. —2 Corinthians 8:21

South Carolina rolled into Jordan-Hare Stadium ranked twelfth, while the Tigers had cracked the top twenty and stood at seventeenth in the nation.

Auburn was still riding a high after a 27–24 overtime win against Clemson.

Cam Newton was grabbing headlines, and college fans all over the country were taking note and wondering whether or not Auburn was for real.

The quarterback from Atlanta, Georgia, ran fifty-four yards to put Auburn on the board 7–0 with six minutes and ten seconds to play in the first period.

The Gamecocks responded and whipped of twenty unanswered points to jump out in front by thirteen.

With forty-six seconds to play in the first half, Newton scored on a four-yard run to close the game to 20–14.

The Tigers took the lead 21–20 when Newton crossed the goal line from three yards out, but South Carolina came back and scored to take a 27–21 lead into the final period.

Auburn wasted little time and put points on the board in the opening moments of the fourth quarter when Newton connected with Philip Lutzenkirchen on a seven-yard touchdown strike.

The Tiger defense stiffened and held the Gamecocks, while Newton connected with Emory Blake for a twelve-yard touchdown pass and the 35–27 lead.

The signal caller finished with 158 yards passing and completed sixteen of his twenty-one attempts (76 percent). He added 176 yards on the ground to go along with his three touchdowns.

Auburn was 4–0 and would be ranked in the top ten the next week. Fans were excited with the anticipation that Newton and his teammates were about to stumble onto something great.

The Tigers were a serious contender and earned the nation's attention.

Are you the real deal? Does your life represent who you stand for?

> Do not lie to one another, seeing that you have put off
> the old self with its practices. —Colossians 3:9

WAR EAGLE

How do people in your neighborhood perceive you? If you claim to be a Christian, do those around you know about it? Or is there some doubt about who you follow? Do they see you do things that leave them scratching their heads in disbelief that you claim to serve God? Your actions matter to your family, friends, and neighbors. Perhaps you have the opinion that what other people think about you is not important—that is not true. It does matter—especially if you represent the Lord.

RIDE FOR THE BRAND

You want to have a positive image in your community and make people aware of your values and convictions. If you tell others you have been born again, but your life shows otherwise, the fallout will damage your testimony. The last word you want someone to use to describe you is "hypocrite." Here are some things to consider when you want to show others you are a genuine follower of Christ:

➢ How You Talk: When someone confronts you or criticizes you in public, the natural response is to fire back and defend yourself. This is even more the case if you are falsely accused of something you did not do. Try your best to resist the temptation to engage in an argument, especially if you are upset and in the heat of the moment. Choose your words carefully, and don't talk out of anger. This is also the case when you are in public with friends or even at home with your family. Words matter, and what you feel in your heart will come out of your mouth. As the old children's song goes, "Oh, be careful, little tongue, what you say." "Whoever keeps his mouth and his tongue keeps himself out of trouble" (Proverbs 21:23).

➢ The Way You Live: Don't be seen in places you know will hurt your witness. Make sure you dress appropriately, and live an honest and upright life. When you wear the brand of Christian, people who are not believers will closely watch what you do and how you conduct yourself to see if you really are who you say you are. They expect you to be an ambassador for the Lord. Don't embarrass His name and give people a reason not to want to live for Him. "Keep your conduct among the Gentiles honorable, so that when they speak against you as evildoers, they may see your good deeds and glorify God on the day of visitation" (1 Peter 2:12).

➢ Who You Associate With: The people you hang out with can make or break your reputation within the community. This does not mean you should never associate with nonbelievers, but your Christian life will grow if you nurture friendships with people who share your values and beliefs. If you are seen often with people who have negative reputations, you might earn one too with guilt by association. You must be the light and the example others want to follow. "Do not be deceived: 'Bad company ruins good morals'" (1 Corinthians 15:33).

➢ How You Give Back: As a follower of the Lord, you are called and encouraged to give back. God expects you to tithe to your local church, and He may ask you to go the extra mile and donate to charities. You should consider donating your extra time and money to causes that are worthwhile and give you an opportunity to spread the love of God to others.

➢ The Way You Worship: Nonbelievers are not the only ones watching you; those you attend church with will also

Day 31: Be a Real Christian

take note. You are not in a popularity contest and should never worship and praise God to be seen and admired. But others can tell if your worship is genuine or fake and only for show, and God can too. You should strive for a testimony of integrity. When your name is mentioned to others in your congregation, will they describe you as dedicated and someone who takes your relationship with the Lord seriously? Be faithful to regular attendance, and go to special services and revivals throughout the year. Do not make it possible for you to be considered a visitor in your own church.

The way you live your life in front of others will be the example to those who are searching to fill their empty hearts. You can also be an inspiration and encouragement to those who share your faith. Show the world that your God is real, and so are you.

DAY 32
ESTABLISH YOURSELF

November 30, 2013: Auburn 34, Alabama 28

That you may be mindful of the words which were spoken before by the holy prophets, and of the commandment of us, the apostles of the Lord and Savior. —2 Peter 3:2 NKJV

The game had it all for Auburn fans.

They witnessed a ninety-nine-yard touchdown pass, a blocked field goal, and a 109-yard game-winning field goal return to win the contest.

But the best part is that it was a victory for the fourth-ranked Tigers over top-ranked Alabama to claim the Iron Bowl.

The Tide rolled into Jordan-Hare Stadium with the stingiest defense in college football.

Auburn's running back Tre Mason did not pay attention to the reputation of Alabama's defense and instead churned out 164 yards on twenty-nine carries (5.6 average per carry).

The product of Lake Worth, Florida, highlighted his performance with two magnificent runs on a game-tying drive in the final quarter.

Throughout the game, college football fans took note that Mason had developed into a legitimate Heisman Trophy candidate.

He moved past legendary running back Bo Jackson on the single-season touchdown mark and established himself as an all-time great football player at Auburn.

How have you established yourself spiritually? Are you a leader or a follower? Are you content to sit back and take it all in, or are you the type who needs to be on the front lines?

Have you set the mark as a person who evangelizes and leads others to the Lord?

Be diligent to present yourself approved to God, a worker who does not need to be ashamed, rightly dividing the word of truth. —2 Timothy 2:15 NKJV

WAR EAGLE

You are expected to evangelize in your Christian journey. You might spread the word in simple and quiet ways, while others shout it from the pulpits throughout the land. You may have a desire to share the good news using an avenue that is unique to you, while effective to those around you. Some people might only think of evangelism as crusades similar to those held by Billy Graham for many years. He saw millions come to the Lord through his efforts. But not everyone is called or equipped to do this type of ministry. But deep down you have a desire to be the witness that others around you need you to be.

RIDE FOR THE BRAND

Maybe you go to church and live a solid Christian life, but you want something more. You feel a calling to step out on faith and demonstrate a bold testimony to lead others to the Lord. You

Day 32: Establish Yourself

want God to use you in your community to be a light in a dark world. Here are some tips for you to consider when you know you are supposed to step up your game:

➤ Step Out of Your Comfort Zone: You may be perfectly comfortable in your own bubble. Maybe you prefer to stay within the confines of a small group of like-minded people or a family environment. This is fine, but sometimes God calls you to think out of the box and venture out to let others know about His mercy and grace. You don't have to be on television or host a radio program, but you can do some great work with small groups of people such as youth sports or Bible studies. Tell others you will meet for prayer before work or practice and see who shows up. Do something different. "Go therefore and make disciples of all the nations, baptizing them in the name of the Father and of the Son and of the Holy Spirit" (Matthew 28:19 NKJV).

➤ Invite Others to Church: Most people are honored when they receive invitations because they make them feel special. Invites to weddings and other special occasions lead you to believe your friendship is valued and people like to be around you. You also entertain feelings of obligation because someone took the time to think of you. As a follower of Christ, take time to contact your friends and family and invite them to church. You don't have to make them feel guilty, but instead make them curious enough to want to come. Be enthusiastic, and let them know it could change their life in the best way possible.

➤ Share Your Experiences: You can evangelize much easier now that social media is available to spread the word. Put out a tweet or post a Bible verse on Facebook a few times a week. All your friends and followers will be exposed to your message. Write a blog or send a letter to the editor. People love to read or be exposed to messages of hope and encouragement. You can be the tool God uses to share the good news. "Come and hear, all you who fear God, and I will declare what He has done for my soul" (Psalm 66:16 NKJV).

➤ Be Hospitable: When you are courteous to strangers, they will often respond positively. This might initiate a conversation and give you the opportunity to explain why you put the needs of others before your own. A word of encouragement and a bright smile are contagious, and genuine kindness goes a long way to show God's love to others.

➤ Pray for Opportunities: Ask God in the stillness of your prayer room to open doors for you to share the gospel. You might be surprised at the unique ways He might lead you to witness for the kingdom. Be open and willing to prepare for the tasks He gives you. If you ask and believe, He will provide.

You don't have to grab the headlines to establish yourself as an effective witness for the Lord. Ask the Master for the chance to shine and follow where He leads.

DAY 33
SHARE YOUR FAITH

November 30, 1957: Auburn 40, Alabama 0

That is, they we may be mutually encouraged by each other's faith, both yours and mine. —Romans 1:12

The Auburn Tigers finished the 1957 campaign with a perfect 10–0 record under Coach Ralph "Shug" Jordan.

The final game of the season featured Alabama in the Iron Bowl at Legion Field in Birmingham.

Auburn dominated all aspects of the game and won 40–0, and many speculated the score could have been worse if the Tigers had not turned the ball over a few times.

They posted a 34–0 lead at the break and had the game under control.

On the ground, the Tigers romped for 237 yards while the defense held Bama to ninety-two. The Tigers also had a slight edge in the air with 106 yards compared to 105 from the Tide.

The lopsided victory was the first Southeastern Conference Championship the Tigers had claimed.

After the contest, the Associated Press, who had ranked the Tigers number one, named Auburn as the National Champions even though the team was on probation from the previous season and did not play in a bowl game.

The Coaches Poll selected Ohio State as National Champions as the Buckeyes posted a 9–1 season record but defeated Oregon 10–7 in the Rose Bowl in Pasadena, California.

Both Auburn and Ohio State shared the title of 1957 National Champion.

Are you confident enough in your faith to share it with others?

Do you take advantage of opportunities to tell your friends about God's saving grace and mercy?

> And that repentance for the forgiveness of sins should be proclaimed in his name to all nations, beginning from Jerusalem. —Luke 24:47

WAR EAGLE

When you share the gospel with others, consider that this may be the first time they have heard about the plan of salvation. This may be your one and only opportunity, so you need to make it good. Share your testimony about the life God rescued you from, and let them know about the peace and joy that comes with having Christ live in your heart. Maybe a coworker has had a bad experience with people in the past who claimed to be Christians but let them down or treated them badly. Help them to see His light in you and quote Scripture that backs up your story. Offer to pray with them, but if they turn you down, let them know you will continue to keep them in your prayers, and offer to answer any questions they might have later.

RIDE FOR THE BRAND

Make up your mind, and focus your efforts on being a positive example of what a team player for God looks like. You may be the only Bible those around you read each day. Be a beacon of light in a dark world, and show others how much you love the Lord. Your positive attitude will attract people. Be aware of situations around you, and don't push your beliefs on others, but demonstrate a loving and caring personality, and be a witness for the Master everywhere you go. Here are some tips on how to share your faith with those around you:

➤ Share Your Experience: When you share your personal story about how God delivered you from sin and unhappiness, others may be able to relate. Your experience is unique and can have an impact on those around you. Let them know how much Christ has made your life worth living. Tell them about the joy and peace in your heart, and make sure they know that God can do the same for them.

➤ Stay Away from Debates: If you engage a person who wants to argue or debate religion with you, stay focused on the message that Jesus saved you and changed your life forever. Avoid discussions about doctrine, and focus the topic on God's love. Tell others about what Jesus did for you personally.

➤ Do Not Complicate the Moment: The plan of salvation is simple. Jesus was born of a virgin, lived a sinless life, performed miracles, was crucified on the Cross, and rose on the third day to make a way for you and me to live with

Him in heaven. Memorize verses from the Bible that explain how to be saved, and share them with others. "For the Son of Man came to seek and to save the lost" (Luke 19:10).

➢ Be Open: Never be disingenuous or inauthentic. Be honest and open about how God delivered you without showing judgment or making others feel uncomfortable. Everyone has sinned and needs forgiveness. Let them know God loves them no matter what they have done and will forgive them of all sins if they call on His name. Show them mercy and grace, and let them know that Jesus has provided a better way to live for all who will accept Him.

➢ Live Your Testimony: Avoid anything that will make others view you as a hypocrite and weaken your testimony. If you stand for the Lord, then never put yourself in a compromising position to let others down. Put your words and faith into action, and be a positive and encouraging example to those around you. "Preach the word; be ready in season and out of season; reprove, rebuke, and exhort, with complete patience and teaching" (2 Timothy 4:2).

When the 1957 season was over, Auburn had produced a perfect season. But they were on probation due to mistakes from the previous season and were not allowed to play in a bowl game. Some saw fit to still name them as national champs, but the Buckeyes were also chosen by a different organization to have the crown. Both were deemed the best in the land and shared the National Championship. You can share your crown too.

DAY 34
BREAK THROUGH THE LINE

December 2, 1972: Auburn 17, Alabama 16

If you faint in the day of adversity, your strength is small. —Proverbs 24:10

With ten minutes left to play in the Iron Bowl, Alabama held a commanding 16–0 lead at Legion Field.

The Tide was ranked second in the nation, boasted a 10–0 record, and was a fourteen-point favorite to win the game.

For the first three quarters, Auburn (8–1) was stymied and dominated by Alabama.

The Tigers managed to kick a field goal with less than ten minutes to play to make the score 16–3.

Some Auburn fans in the stands were frustrated and booed the decision to boot the ball through the uprights instead of going for a touchdown.

Alabama's next offensive drive stalled, and they were forced to punt.

The Tide was deep in its own territory on fourth down when Auburn's Bill Newton broke through the line and blocked the punt.

David Langner scooped up the ball and rumbled into the end zone from twenty-five yards out to make the score 16–10.

Auburn had new life, and Alabama became nervous.

The Tigers again forced another three-and-out, and the punting unit came onto the field for the Tide.

But just like before, the duo of Newton and Langner combined for another score and blocked the punt again for the 17–16 lead.

Alabama had one final drive to try to win the game, but Langner picked off a Tide pass to secure the win.

The game is considered one of the greatest comebacks in Auburn history.

Newton broke through the offensive line and blocked two punts in a row, and Langner scored touchdowns both times. What are the odds of that happening again?

Do you need to break through from the guilt or shame that holds you back?

You can block the devil's punt and make your comeback to serve the Lord.

> When I am afraid, I put my trust in you. In God, whose word I praise, in God I trust; I shall not be afraid. What can flesh do to me? —Psalm 56:3–4

WAR EAGLE

Everyone faces obstacles and spiritual battles along their journey. You invite some by your own actions while others may blindside you. You may have decided to follow the Lord, but you still entertain feelings of guilt and shame from your past. Perhaps you are trying to move on, but the devil creeps into your thoughts at night and whispers that you cannot be forgiven for the things you have done.

RIDE FOR THE BRAND

Satan may have you down on the scoreboard with an apparent victory in hand. He might be ready to celebrate your defeat and stomp you into the ground. But just when all hope is lost, God sends His angels to help you charge the offensive line and break through to block the punt. You might be in a position that seems hopeless and you face the bitter taste of defeat. But don't give up hope; God will not only help you block the kick, He will help you come through in the clutch. Do you need to hear from Christ? Will He come through at just the right time? Fear can be a powerful intruder in your life if you allow the forces of evil to stack the line. Here are some ways to battle the fear and allow God to lead you to victory:

➤ Line Up in the Word: No college football team players ignore their playbook. Inside, they find strategy and options to score and defeat their opponent. You have the ultimate playbook at your disposal and must use it every day. Inside, you will find the wonderful and magnificent designs the Lord has prepared for you to bust through the line and block the punt. Read it daily and find encouragement and inspiration. "Your word is a lamp to my feet and a light to my path" (Psalm 119:105).

➤ Take Note of the Lies from the Enemy: When Satan whispers that you are not loved or that no one cares about you, draw close to the One who created you. Remember that you are His child, and He loves you so much that He sent Jesus, His only Son, to die on the Cross for you.

Don't let falsehoods make you bitter and tempt you to leave your faith. Fall back on God's love for you.

➢ Focus on the Truth from God: The truth will always set you free. People find it easy to believe a lie while it seems the truth must always be investigated and proven. God's love is amazing because it's been proven time and again. He will never leave you to taste defeat. "And you will know the truth, and the truth will set you free" (John 8:32).

➢ Find Your Courage: Rebuke the lies from the devil and live in the freedom and peace God wants you to enjoy. Stand up to the enemy and break through the line in the fourth quarter to block the punt and score the go-ahead touchdown. "The wicked flee when no one pursues, but the righteous are bold as a lion" (Proverbs 28:1).

➢ Praise the Play: When the touchdowns were scored to win the game, players and fans jumped for joy and celebrated the conference win. When the Lord comes through for you, He deserves your praise. Let Him know how much you appreciate His goodness. Tell others about how the Lord blocked the punt and allowed you to score. Lift your arms in honor and praise and even shout to the top of the stadium if you feel the urge. Celebrate the win.

Just when the game looks hopeless and defeat is near, reach down deep and focus on what God has done for you in the past. Fight through the discouragement, and let God make back-to-back defensive plays to lead you to the upset win.

DAY 35
PROTECT AGAINST THE BLIND-SIDE HIT

November 13, 2004: Auburn 24, Georgia 6

Watch and pray, that ye enter not into temptation; the spirit indeed is willing, but the flesh is weak.
—Matthew 26:41 KJV

Both teams were ranked in the top ten in the nation, and the game had major bowl implications for the winner.

Auburn controlled the contest and enjoyed a 17–0 lead in the third quarter.

The Tigers threatened to score again, but quarterback Jason Campbell's pass in the end zone was picked by a Georgia defender.

The Bulldogs put together a drive to post a score and get back into the game.

Georgia had the ball at the Auburn twenty-eight-yard line on third down when quarterback David Greene spotted wide receiver Reggie Brown open across the middle.

Brown hauled in the pass for what appeared to be a first down grab.

But Auburn safety Junior Rosegreen moved in on Brown like a torpedo and hit the receiver hard enough to jar the ball loose and cause a fumble.

Will Herring recovered the pigskin for Auburn and stopped the drive and any attempt by Georgia to score a touchdown and get back into the game.

The receiver suffered a concussion and did not return to the game.

Today, the hit might be considered "targeting," but it was not a dirty play from Rosegreen. It was just a hard football hit from a defender.

The Tigers went on to win 24–6 and finished the season undefeated at 13–0, which included the Southeastern Conference Championship and a Sugar Bowl title.

Have you ever been knocked out by the devil? Has he hit you hard enough to jar your faith loose and cause you to fumble?

There are many ways the forces of evil will attack you. One of the best tools he uses is social media and the Internet. He will use these to come across the middle right when you think you are going to gain the first down and blindside you with a dirty hit.

> But every man is tempted, when he is drawn away of his own lust, and enticed. —James 1:14 KJV

WAR EAGLE

The devil does not play fair and will resort to any tactic he can to ruin your life. One of the most well used weapons he has at his disposal is social media. Most people use social media to post pictures and catch up with friends, but the devil has other purposes in mind. While many Christians use these platforms to help and encourage others, the enemy uses them to trick you with temptation.

RIDE FOR THE BRAND

You are home alone and trying to meet a deadline for work when you come across a provocative profile you have never seen. Or you receive a friend request from an attractive lady you don't know. Or you have a follower who wants to send you a message and you know better, but you accept it. These things can happen if you let your guard down. Satan wants to use social media to achieve the following:

➤ He Wants to Destroy Your Marriage: What begins with an occasional like now and then develops into more. An innocent interaction leads to a private conversation and then a personal encounter. Before you know what has hit you—just like Reggie Brown—you fumble the ball. A platonic "friendship" has turned into an emotional or physical affair. You can take precautions by having a joint account with your spouse or sharing passwords with each other. Protect each other's backs. Allow your spouse to have access to your media accounts, and don't hide anything. If you keep a post or picture hidden from your spouse, you should not have it in the first place. Your marriage and the family are the main targets of the devil.

➤ He Wants to Control Your Thoughts: From time to time, it's a good idea to take a break from social media. A dangerous practice for a Christian is to scroll endlessly to waste time. Eventually, you will come across temptation and fall into the trap of the enemy. Never entertain the notion that you are too strong for the devil and you won't fall for his tricks. He is sneaky and knows your vulnerabilities. Your "little secret" is the worst thing you can have. It takes strength and courage to unfollow or unfriend others once you realize that your thoughts are not what or where they should be. "Blessed are the pure in heart; for they shall see God" (Matthew 5:8 KJV).

➢ He Wants to Dominate Your Time: Have you ever scrolled through social media while on the job or tried to have a conversation with a person who keeps glancing at their phone? Have you ever been awake at night and jumped on social media to see what others are doing? The devil wants you to allow his distractions to lure you into trouble. This doesn't mean that all social media is bad, but when it's all you think about, Satan has you right where he wants you. Take a break, especially when you are with your family and friends. Don't be rude. Find the lost art of exchanging words in a dialogue over coffee. If you are out to dinner with your spouse, focus on them and leave your phone off.

➢ He Wants to Take Away from Your Devotional Time: What comes first when you wake up in the morning? Social media or your daily devotions? The devil wants you to focus on *you* through social media. But your day will start out so much better with a cup of coffee and the

Word of God. Put the Lord first and focus on spending time with Him first before checking out what the rest of the world is doing.

➢ He Wants to Wreck Your Image: Fake accounts are common, and people will believe a lie faster than the truth. Be careful what you like and how you comment on a friend's page. Your intentions can be taken out of context, and your image can be tarnished. "Neither give place to the devil" (Ephesians 4:27 KJV).

There are several bad scenarios that can play out, and you must be on guard. Social media can be a fun and effective way to spread the gospel and help you to enjoy connecting with friends and family. But it is also a tool used by the devil to try to destroy you. Make the catch over the middle, and swivel your head to see who is coming in to knock you out in an effort to make you fumble your reputation and ruin your life.

DAY 36

HOW IS YOUR RELATIONSHIP WITH GOD?

November 11, 2017: Auburn 40, Georgia 17

> For we are his workmanship, created in Christ Jesus for good works, which God prepared beforehand, that we should walk in them. —Ephesians 2:10

The only way to beat number-one ranked Georgia was to control the line of scrimmage.

Auburn was an underdog to the undefeated Bulldogs and ranked tenth in the nation with a record of 7–2.

A win would increase the Tigers' chances for a major bowl game appearance and knock out the possibility for Georgia to reach the National Championship game. They developed a game plan that worked.

Nick Chubb, the dynamic running back for Georgia surpassed the great Bo Jackson, but this was the only bright spot for the Bulldogs.

Chubb scored one touchdown and gained twenty-seven yards as Auburn's defense stuffed the nation's top team 40–17.

On the other end, Auburn's Kerryon Johnson ran wild for 167 yards on the ground.

Auburn also sacked Georgia's quarterback Jake Fromm four times and pressured him throughout the entire game.

He led his team to a touchdown on the game's first drive but was stifled by the defense for the remainder and only managed another touchdown and a field goal in the third quarter.

The Tigers came into the contest with a game plan and executed it to perfection.

They blew out the top team in the land and conquered the "Deep South's Oldest Rivalry."

The meetings between the two teams over the years have been memorable. The history of this competition dates back to their first meeting in 1892.

There is a family connection—they are separated by less than a three-hour drive, and many Georgia fans live in Alabama and vice-versa. Georgia's all-time winningest coach, Vince Dooley, received his bachelor's and master's degrees from Auburn. He also played for the Tigers under Coach Shug Jordan. Former Auburn coach Pat Dye played football at Georgia. And there are more.

Intensity precedes each game, bragging rights are important to the fans, and the tailgating is legendary.

Home-field advantage does not exist in this rivalry as the visiting team has won more games in this matchup. The competition between the two teams has historically been both exciting and unpredictable.

Has your relationship with the Lord been exciting and unpredictable? Are you blessed to be part of the family of God? Are you intensely devoted to serving Him? Do you have a home-field advantage at your local church?

> I praise you, for I am fearfully and wonderfully made.
> Wonderful are your works; my soul knows it very well.
> —Psalm 139:14

WAR EAGLE

On social media, people often use many different or colorful words to depict their relationship status for others to see. Some use humorous words such as "it's complicated" while others are simpler and more to the point with descriptions like "married," "single," or "interested." These are used to let everyone know if you are available or not to begin a new relationship. You can send the wrong message or fail to convey the correct one to people who see your posts. Some might wonder what your status might be if they see it for the first time.

RIDE FOR THE BRAND

Do you make it obvious to others that you have a relationship with God? Do your family members, coworkers, or fellow students know you are a Christian? Do your actions back up your faith, or do they leave people scratching their heads and wondering about your authenticity? Do the following words adequately describe your relationship status with the Savior?

➤ Are you *approachable?* Are you open and willing to allow the Lord to approach you with His plan for your life? Do others feel comfortable in asking you about your faith? Do they see Jesus in you? Do you keep your faith to yourself or share it with others? "Walk in wisdom toward outsiders, making the best use of the time. Let your speech always be gracious, seasoned with salt, so that you may know how you ought to answer each person" (Colossians 4:5–6).

➤ Do you *behold* God? Do you delight in His presence? Do you wait on His plan? Do you find rest and shelter during a storm? "You make known to me the path of life; in your presence there is fullness of joy; at your right hand are pleasures forevermore" (Psalm 16:11).

➤ Do you seek *holiness*? Do you meditate in prayer and call on His name? Do you find the Word of God nourishing to your soul? Do you cry out to the Lord in prayer and seek His will? Do you go through the motions, or is your salvation heartfelt? "And whatever we ask we receive from him, because we keep his commandments and do what pleases him" (1 John 3:22).

➤ How are you *perceived*? Are you humble? Do you listen to the Lord and obey His commands? Do your actions reflect a genuine relationship with your Heavenly Father? Are you a beacon of hope to others? "The reward for humility and fear of the LORD is riches and honor and life" (Proverbs 22:4).

➤ Do you *worship*? Do you cast your cares upon Him? Do you sing His praises and honor God? Do you take the time to thank Him for all the blessings He has bestowed on you? Do you find strength when you exalt the name of Jesus? "God is spirit, and those who worship him must worship in spirit and truth" (John 4:24).

Fans love the Auburn-Georgia rivalry because it has it all. Does your relationship with God have it all, or is there something missing? How would others depict your life as a believer in the Lord Jesus Christ? Ask God to reveal any shortcomings, and ask Him to help you fix them and make needed improvements. Live your life so there is no question that you are a true follower of God.

DAY 37
RETIRE YOUR NUMBER

October 31, 1992: Auburn 24, Arkansas 24

For you were bought with a price. So glorify God in your body. —1 Corinthians 6:20

Although the contest between Auburn and Arkansas was important, it was just an afterthought.

The Tigers and Razorbacks battled to a 24–24 tie game in Pat Dye's twelfth season.

But if you ask the Auburn faithful what happened that day, they might not remember the game or the score. They probably remember best that it was the day a football legend was enshrined forever, and his number was retired by the university.

This was Bo Jackson's day, and his number thirty-four was put behind glass and displayed for all to see. No one at Auburn will ever wear that jersey again.

Jackson was a remarkable athlete who excelled at football, baseball, and track at Auburn.

In 1985, he dismantled defenses and averaged an amazing 6.4 yards per carry. He earned 1,786 yards and scored seventeen touchdowns, leading the Tigers to an 8–4 record and an appearance in the Cotton Bowl.

The same year, he led the nation in yards rushing, average per carry, touchdowns, and yards per game.

When his career at Auburn ended, he had posted a total of 4,575 all-purpose yards and forty-five touchdowns, and he averaged 6.6 yards per carry.

In 1985, he won the Heisman Trophy and the Walter Camp Award. He was also selected as the *Sporting News* Player of the Year and the UPI Player of the Year. Jackson was a two-time consensus All-American and a three-time First-Team All-SEC player.

He combined grace and power when he ran the football.

Although he never played on a National Championship team, Jackson is regarded as one of the best college-football running backs to have ever played the game.

For his efforts, Auburn honored his dedication and accomplishments.

What about your Christian journey? Will you have your jersey number retired? Will you do anything to seal your spiritual legacy?

I give thanks to you, O Lord my God, with my whole heart, and I will glorify your name forever. —Psalm 86:12

WAR EAGLE

You know what success looks like and how to reach it by now. During your childhood, your parents hopefully taught you to play by the rules, work hard, and mind your own business. Serving God does not exempt you from battling obstacles in life, but if you put God first, you have a magnificent chance to win the big game. Perhaps during your childhood, you were encouraged to attend church and Sunday school regularly, say your bedtime prayers, and trust in the Lord to take care of you. Maybe you have done your best to live by the Golden Rule and have personified a life of honesty. As a Christian, what can you expect when your life is over?

RIDE FOR THE BRAND

Auburn plays each year with the hope of winning the conference title. Of course they would also like to win the National Championship, but that won't be accomplished if they cannot claim to be the best in the Southeastern Conference. As a follower of Christ, your only mission is to reach heaven no matter the cost. Your focus is on the Lord, and you must ask Him to help you as you face both the good and bad times. Bo Jackson ran on a mission to be the best player in college football. He reached that milestone when he was chosen to receive the Heisman Trophy. A few years later, his number was retired to honor his legacy at Auburn. Here are some ways you can keep your eyes on the prize and win heaven's most prestigious award. Once you try these suggestions and make them part of your routine, these habits will draw you closer to a more obedient life in Christ, which is evidence of your faith:

➤ Spend Quality Time with God: Reading the Bible and praying regularly are both important steps on the way to eternity and are vital to your spiritual success. But you can strive to go even deeper. Memorize as much Scripture as you can, and use it in your prayers. This also comes in handy when you are under attack from Satan. Keep notes from devotions that speak to you, and review them as often as possible to help strengthen your walk with Christ. Pray throughout the day, and ask for God's help in all things, no matter how big or small.

➤ Practice an Attitude of Gratitude: Make a point to be truly thankful to God for all your blessings. Don't take His love and salvation for granted. Try writing down three different things you are grateful for each day for the next three months. This will help you to put your blessings into perspective and realize just how good He is to you and your family. A grateful heart will draw you closer to the Lord. "Thanks be to God for his inexpressible gift!" (2 Corinthians 9:15).

➤ Give Way to God's Plans for Your Life: Everyone should have personal and professional goals. You might go to college to train for a certain occupation and join organizations that will help to develop your character and integrity. But what happens when Christ tells you to do something different and sets you on the opposite path? You must pray and ask Him for guidance and direction. Examine your shortcomings, and be willing to make changes to honor His leading. He is not the author of confusion but will lead you down a clear path of joy and peace to help you fulfill His plans for your future.

➤ Serve Others: When you give of your money and time, you are giving back to others the blessings God has given you. You are to be a positive example and help others in need around you. Giving your money is admirable, but it means even more when you take a step further and give the most valuable commodity you have—your time. Instead of sleeping in on a Saturday, wake up early and volunteer at a soup kitchen or be a Big Brother or Big Sister to a young person. "Whoever is generous to the poor lends to the LORD, and he will repay him for his deed" (Proverbs 19:17).

➢ Honor the Lord in His House: Those who are hit-or-miss when it comes to church attendance will not reach the full potential God has for them. What would have happened if Bo Jackson only showed up for half the games Auburn played? Would he have reached the milestones he did? No. He put in his time at practice and was ready on game day. You must do the same. Show up when the church doors are open, and be active and participate.

Bo Jackson worked hard. He combined his God-given abilities with a determined work ethic. He paid the price for success and was rewarded for his efforts. You can also do this in your Christian life. Pray hard, live for God, stay in His Word, and follow His plan for your life, and you will receive your reward in heaven.

DAY 38
LAUGH MORE

November 7, 1896: Auburn 45, Georgia Tech 0

Be glad in the LORD, and rejoice, O righteous, and shout for joy, all you upright in heart! —Psalm 32:11

The incident that inspired the "Wreck Tech Pajama Parade" did not actually happen during this game—it happened beforehand.

A group of naughty cadets from Auburn wanted to impress the engineers from Georgia Tech who had a reputation for their knowledge of science.

The group sneaked out of the dorms the night before the big game between Auburn and Georgia Tech and applied grease to the railroad tracks that led into Auburn.

When the train carrying the Georgia Tech football team arrived, it could not get stopped at its destination to let the team off the train. Instead, it kept going until it was halfway to the next town of Loachapoka, Alabama.

When the train finally stopped, the players on board were forced to walk about five miles back to Auburn with all their gear.

Auburn dominated the game and won 45–0.

While the cadets never greased the tracks again, *USA Today* called the joke the second-best college football prank in history.

The practical joke motivated a tradition years later that did not involve grease or train tracks. In 1988, students constructed floats and walked the streets in their pajamas as part of the "Wreck Tech Pajama Parade" through downtown Auburn. In 2003 and 2005, the ritual caught steam again when Georgia Tech added Auburn to its schedule.

The ingenious prank committed almost one hundred years earlier most likely drew a lot of laughs, except from the players who had to walk the five miles before playing a football game.

We all need to laugh and have fun. Laughter is great medicine for those who take life way too seriously.

A good laugh and a broad smile have its benefits.

Do you think Christians should never bust a gut or pull a joke on someone?

All the days of the afflicted are evil, but the cheerful of heart has a continual feast. —Proverbs 15:15

WAR EAGLE

As Christians, we need to have fun and enjoy this gift from God in our lives. Even God has a sense of humor, and He does not intend for our spiritual life to be stuffy. He wants us to have joy in serving Him. If we take life too seriously and never show those around us how happy we are, they will not be attracted to serving Christ.

RIDE FOR THE BRAND

Joking around and having fun has its place in the church and in your personal life. While being serious about your relationship with God, your work, and your family is important, laughter is a gift from God to lighten our Christian journey. Too many people are too serious and get offended way too easily. We should all lighten up and enjoy the spiritual benefits of laughter:

> Humor Creates Humility: It takes a humble heart to chuckle at yourself and at some of the hilarious things you do every day. When you can giggle at your own actions, you kick any traces of pride through the end zone and out of bounds. There is no room for an ego when you are a follower of Christ. Laugh more in life, especially at yourself. "When pride comes, then comes disgrace, but with the humble is wisdom" (Proverbs 11:2).

> Laughter Keeps You Grounded: You are surrounded with depressing and scary news every time you turn on the television. Comedy can keep you interested in life after you have been bombarded with negative news from all over the world. You need to know what is going on every day, but you also need an escape from all the craziness. A good sense of humor will help keep your life in perspective. "A joyful heart is good medicine, but a crushed spirit dries up the bones" (Proverbs 17:22).

> A Sense of Humor Can Heal Your Mind and Body: Laughter can relieve built-up stress from the hustle and bustle of the world and can serve as an outlet for your emotions. Humor

can help alleviate a tense moment or bring a smile during a time of trial. There are moments in life when you need to focus on what is important, but a well-timed laugh or grin can help loosen things up and make it easier to cope.

➢ Laughter Can Chase Away Fear: When you can enjoy your life in Christ and laugh with your friends and family, you enjoy freedom. Show the devil that he cannot take away your joy. You are a child of the King, and you have a reason to be happy.

➢ A Smile Is Welcoming: A person who smiles or laughs a lot is often the most popular person in the room. Why? Because laughter is contagious. People are drawn like a moth to the light. When you smile and make others feel at ease with a laugh, they can let their guard down around you. This might open the door for you to witness about why you smile and laugh. You might get the opportunity to share with them about the love of God in your heart. "A glad heart makes a cheerful face, but by sorrow of heart the spirit is crushed" (Proverbs 15:13).

The prank the Auburn cadets pulled off was classic and timeless. It alleviated some pressure and made some people laugh. Now that so many years have passed, hopefully the Georgia Tech fans can now appreciate the effort too. Laughter in the right time and place can be a wonderful tool for you to use to show the world you are a Christian.

DAY 39
BE READY TO COVER THE KICK

January 3, 2005: Auburn 16, Virginia Tech 13

The preparations of the heart in man, and the answer in tongue, is from the LORD. —Proverbs 16:1 KJV

Auburn needed to make a strong statement to be in consideration for the National Championship debate.

The Tigers, who faced Virginia Tech in the 2005 Sugar Bowl in New Orleans, got on the board early after John Vaughn kicked a twenty-one-yard field goal in the opening drive for the 3–0 lead.

The pass from Hokies quarterback Bryan Randall was picked off by Junior Rosegreen, which put Auburn in good field position.

Another boot from Vaughn extended the lead to 6–0.

Virginia Tech threatened in the second quarter and had the ball at the Auburn two-yard line.

Randall's fourth-down pass to Jesse Allen fell in the end zone, and Auburn took over on their own one-yard line.

Instead of taking a potential 7–6 lead, Virginia Tech had to play defense.

But Auburn orchestrated an offensive drive that went ninety-two yards to the Tech seven-yard line. Vaughn came in to kick another field goal for the 9–0 lead at the break.

The Tigers picked up where they left off in the third period and put together another impressive drive. Quarterback Jason Campbell connected with Anthony Mix for a fifty-three-yard pass completion that took the ball inside the Red Zone.

From there, running back Devin Aromashodu plowed in from five yards out for the 16–0 advantage.

On Auburn's next possession, the Hokies forced a fumble, which set up a twenty-nine-yard touchdown pass from Randall to Josh Morgan.

The duo hooked up again as the game clock wound down for an eighty-yard touchdown strike with just over two minutes to play. Just like that, Virginia Tech was back in the game and trailed by three points.

But they needed the ball back.

They tried an on-side kick, but Auburn's Cooper Wallace was in position to secure the pigskin and the win for the Tigers.

He was prepared to make the play.

Are you ready to defend against the devil's strategy to defeat you?

> Commit thy works unto the LORD, and thy thoughts shall be established. —Proverbs 16:3 KJV

WAR EAGLE

Your Christian journey should be about focusing on God's game plan for your life so you can reach heaven. Throughout your race, you have celebrated major wins, but you have also faced some difficult challenges. The devil wants you to focus on the negatives and give up. He is relentless in his pursuit to force you to fumble. He will use personal tragedies and throw situations at you that might be tough to handle as he works to try to catch you unprepared.

RIDE FOR THE BRAND

You are determined to win the Sugar Bowl and hoist the trophy at the end of the game. You might enjoy a solid lead right now, but you cannot afford to let down your guard. The forces of evil will always try to make a comeback and attempt the on-side kick to retain possession and score the go-ahead touchdown. But you must always anticipate trickery and be ready to fall on the ball once it's kicked to you. Here are some areas where you need to be ready:

➢ Be Prepared to Praise Him: God loves it when you honor and worship Him. He deserves it because He sent His only Son to die for your sins so you could live with Him forever in heaven. You should not only praise Him in the good times but even when life appears to be bleak. He will never leave you or forsake you, no matter what on-side kick attempt you face. Praise Him. "O come, let us worship and bow down: let us kneel before the LORD our maker" (Psalm 95:6 KJV).

➢ Be Prepared to Face Trials: You will face challenges throughout life. There are no guarantees that everything will be rosy all the time. But it's how you handle adversity that makes you strong. Your faith might be persecuted, or you might have to endure personal health issues. No matter what long pass the devil throws at you, be ready to lean on the Lord to allow you to cover the on-side kick. "And not only so, but we glory in tribulations also: knowing that tribulation worketh patience" (Romans 5:3 KJV).

➢ Be Prepared to Share the Gospel: If you are a member of the Lord's team, you must always be ready to share the good news. You don't have to be a minister to do this. You can tell others about the Master in your everyday life and let your light shine with a smile. But when it comes down to the final play of the game, you should always be ready to help others find their way to the Cross.

➢ Be Prepared to Be Happy: Life is too short to be unhappy. God made a way for you to spend eternity with Him—this is reason enough to be happy. Wear a smile and don't dwell on the negative things that happen to you. Instead, focus on the good things Christ has done for you. Be happy and cover the kick.

➢ Be Prepared to Meet the Lord: This is the most important. At the end of the game, you want to be on the winning team. You must surrender yourself to the Lord and ask Him to forgive you of your sins. This is the ultimate prize. Obey His directions, pray every day, and read the Gospels. Follow His commandments, and worship Him in church. Be ready to meet Him.

Cooper Wallace fell on the squibbed kick and ensured the victory for Auburn. He knew what Tech was going to try and kept his eye on the pigskin. He did not lose focus and made sure the ball was secured. You must do the same. Don't take your eyes off God when the game is on the line. Fall on the kicked ball to lock in the victory.

DAY 40
REPLACE THE OAKS

A Happy Place: Toomer's Corner

May the God of hope fill you with all joy and peace in believing, so that by the power of the Holy Spirit you may abound in hope. —Romans 15:13

Most Auburn football fans are familiar with the location and the legacy of Toomer's Corner.

Two streets near the campus of Auburn University— Magnolia Avenue and College Street—intersect and mark the transition from downtown Auburn onto the campus.

Toomer's Corner is named after Alabama State Senator Sheldon Toomer, who also founded Toomer's Drugs at the same corner where the two streets meet.

The drug store has been an institution and a landmark for nearly 130 years.

In 1937, two oak trees were planted, and they grew to be massive and hang over the street corners.

Every time something good and positive happened in town, the corner became a place of celebration.

Back in the day, when Auburn won a football game, fans started a tradition of "rolling" the trees with toilet paper for fun.

A massive celebration took place in 1972 when Auburn beat Alabama in the famous Punt Bama Punt game. The corner and the trees were decorated in toilet paper, and the fans loved every minute.

During football season, it was custom to hold pep rallies on the corner under the big oaks. But in January 2011, an Alabama fan poisoned the trees out of his hatred for Tigers football. Harvey Updyke Jr. was arrested and later convicted of the crime that eventually killed the two trees.

He was fined $1,000 and given a three-year "split sentence" of prison. He served six months in jail and was banned from the Auburn campus.

Updyke was released from jail in 2013, and the following year university officials announced it would plant two full-grown oak trees in the same spot where the originals once stood.

But in 2016, the symbolic trees were attacked again when one was set on fire.

The next year, two new oaks were planted in hopes of restoring the tradition to celebrate an Auburn victory.

> Until now, you have asked nothing in my name. Ask, and you will receive that your joy may be full. —John 16:24

WAR EAGLE

Toomer's Corner has been an important part of the history and proud tradition of Auburn football. Perhaps you have established some important traditions in your life with your church and your family that are part of your Christian journey. But Satan hates to see you consistently serve God and celebrate His presence in your life.

192

RIDE FOR THE BRAND

Your life has come under attack from the devil. He hates you with every ounce of meaning he has in his body. The best thing you can do is let God plant the seed of salvation in your mind and heart. Tear down your dying oaks and replace them with trees that will live forever. Here is how you can make the decision to follow Christ:

➤ Hear the Word: Have you ever been exposed to the gospel at some point in your life? Maybe you visited a Vacation Bible School as a child or heard a sermon on the radio. Perhaps you attended a church service and felt the convicting power of Jesus all around you. Maybe you witnessed a miracle and can't explain what happened. Deep down, you know you need a Savior. Search for a local church where you can learn more about the plan of salvation. "So faith comes from hearing, and hearing through the word of Christ" (Romans 10:17).

➤ Believe the Lord Died for Your Sins: Jesus Christ, the Son of God, came to earth as a baby who was born of a virgin. He lived a perfect life and died on the Cross for the sins of all humankind. He rose three days later and is working today to prepare mansions in heaven for all who believe in eternal life through Him. If you want to accept Him, believe and ask Him to forgive you of your sins and come to live inside your heart. Salvation is that simple. "For God so loved the world, that he gave his only Son, that whoever believes in him should not perish but have eternal life" (John 3:16).

➢ Repent of Your Sins: Everyone has sinned and made mistakes. But once you ask God to forgive you, He will. Then you must make it a priority not to make the same mistake or sin on purpose. "Repent therefore, and turn back, that your sins may be blotted out" (Acts 3:19).

➢ Confess and Ask Him to Save You: After you have acknowledged your transgressions, ask the Lord to save your soul and live in your heart. Be determined to live a righteous life before the Lord and your family and friends. "If we confess our sins, he is faithful and just to forgive us our sins and to cleanse us from all unrighteousness" (1 John 1:9).

➢ Follow God the Rest of Your Life: This will be the best decision ever. You will ensure that you will spend eternity in heaven with the Lord. Making the decision to serve God will give you a better feeling than beating Alabama 75–0. "Commit your way to the LORD; trust in him, and he will act" (Psalm 37:5).

Once you give your life to the Lord, you can celebrate. Why not venture to Toomer's Corner and toss some toilet paper on some trees and let everyone know you are a child of the King? Start your own tradition. Don't turn bitter and allow the devil to poison the trees in your life. Live abundantly through Christ, and let Him give you peace and joy that is mightier than the tallest oak trees at Toomer's Corner. Rest beneath the comforts of the shade of the Tree of Life.

ABOUT THE AUTHOR

Del Duduit is a literary agent with C.Y.L.E. and freelance writer. He is represented by Cyle Young, Hartline Literary Agency and is a member of Serious Writer Inc.

He is the author of *Buckeye Believer: 40 Days of Devotions for the Ohio State Faithful* (2018, BY Books), *Bengal Believer: 40 Who-Dey-Votions for the Cincinnati Faithful* (2019, BY Books), *Dugout Devotions: Inspirational Hits from MLB's Best,* (2019, Iron Stream Books), *First Down Devotions: Inspirations from NFL's Best* (2019, Iron Stream Books), and *Bama Believer: 40 Days of Devotions for the Roll Tide Faithful* (2020, Iron Stream Books).

As a former sportswriter, he won both Associated Press and Ohio Prep Sports writing awards.

In 2016, Del began concentrating more seriously on his passion for writing and building his platform. His weekly blog appears at delduduit.com, and his posts have been retweeted to as many as five million followers through social media across the United States and in two other continents.

Del's articles have appeared in Athletes in Action, *Clubhouse Magazine*, Sports Spectrum, *The Sports Column*, One Christian Voice, *The Christian View* online magazine, and *Portsmouth Metro Magazine*. His blogs have appeared on One Christian Voice and its national affiliates across the country, on ToddStarnes.com and on Almost an Author and *The Write Conversation*.

In 2017, he was named Outstanding Author, first place in short nonfiction, and first place in inspirational at the Ohio Christian Writers Conference. He also won a first place Blue

Seal Award in nonfiction at the 2018 Ohio Christian Writers Conference. In 2019, *Buckeye Believer: 40 Days of Devotions for the Ohio State Faithful* won second place in the Selah Awards for Best Devotional at the Blue Ridge Mountain Christian Writers Conference. His book, *First Down Devotions: Inspirations from NFL's Best*, was nominated as a finalist in the devotional category for the Selah Awards.

He and his wife Angie live in Lucasville, Ohio, and attend Rubyville Community Church.

If you enjoyed this book, will you consider sharing the message with others?

Let us know your thoughts at info@ironstreammedia.com. You can also let the author know by visiting or sharing a photo of the cover on our social media pages or leaving a review at a retailer's site. All of it helps us get the message out!

Facebook.com/IronStreamMedia

Iron Stream Books, New Hope® Publishers, Ascender Books, and New Hope Kidz are imprints of Iron Stream Media, which derives its name from Proverbs 27:17,

"As iron sharpens iron, so one person sharpens another."

This sharpening describes the process of discipleship, one to another. With this in mind, Iron Stream Media provides a variety of solutions for churches, ministry leaders, and nonprofits ranging from in-depth Bible study curriculum and Christian book publishing to custom publishing and consultative services. Through our popular Life Bible Study, Student Life Bible Study brands, and New Hope imprints, ISM provides web-based full-year and short-term Bible study teaching plans as well as printed devotionals, Bibles, and discipleship curriculum.

For more information on ISM and Iron Stream Books, please visit

IronStreamMedia.com

ARTWORK FOR AUBURN AND SEC FANS

IF YOU LIKE THE FRONT COVER OF
AUBURN BELIEVER,
CHECK OUT OTHER PRINTS BY THIS ARTIST.
ALL PRINTS ARE AVAILABLE EXCLUSIVELY FROM THE BEVELED EDGE.

**Order a copy today at
thebevelededgeonline.com**

Search by Artist: Tim Atchenson
Search by Work: Reflections,
SEC, Auburn Prints

About the Artist

The artist, Tim Atchenson, is a twenty-eight-year veteran of the US Army and Alabama Army National Guard. He currently serves as the supervisor for the National Guard recruiting team based in Tuscaloosa, Alabama. He and his wife Shannon live in the Birmingham area, and he graciously acknowledges that he could not pursue his artistic endeavors without her support over the last twenty-one years and counting.